Not Really Hollywood

Not Really Hollywood

Rick Connelly

BearManor Media
2022

Not Really Hollywood

© 2022 Rick Connelly

All rights reserved.

No portion of this publication may be reproduced, stored, and/or copied electronically (except for academic use as a source), nor transmitted in any form or by any means without the prior written permission of the publisher and/or author.

Published in the United States of America by:

BearManor Media

4700 Millenia Blvd.
Suite 175 PMB 90497
Orlando, FL 32839

bearmanormedia.com

Printed in the United States.

Typesetting and layout by BearManor Media

ISBN—978-1-62933-854-5

NOT REALLY HOLLYWOOD

Dedicated to Grandpa Rick's Playmate

Betty (2years old)

Table of Contents

Preface ix

1. It's A Small World 1
2. The Perfect Father 4
3. Beaver's Short Pants 10
4. Cat Out of the Bag 15
5. Boat Builders 17
6. Most Interesting Characters 19
7. Beaver's Freckles 26
8. Eddie's Double Cross 30
9. New Doctor 32
10. Ward's Problem 36
11. Boarding School 41
12. Beaver Sees America 46
13. Beaver's Prep School 50
14. Beaver's Cat Problem 52
15. Beaver's First Date 56
16. Beaver's Newspaper 61
17. Beaver's Bad Day 65
18. Beaver Gets Spelled 70
19. Beaver Plays Hooky 73
20. Beaver Says Goodbye 77
21. Don Juan Beaver 81

22. Wally's Haircomb 84

23. Wally Buys a Car 87

24. Beaver the Caddy 90

25. Lumpy's Car Trouble 94

26. Price of Fame 98

27. Eddie, the Businessman 118

28. Beaver's Ring 122

29. Beaver's Old Friend 127

30. New Neighbors 131

31. Found Money 133

32. Beaver the Magician 138

33. Child Care 144

34. Beaver's Long Night 147

35. Wally's Election 150

36. Beaver's Team 153

37. Beaver Runs Away 156

38. Part-Time Genius 158

39. Beaver's Hero 159

40. Beaver's Office Attraction 160

41. The Grass is Always Greener 164

42. Beaver's Report Card 167

43. Last Day of School 169

Index 172

Preface

Not Really Hollywood is a story about celebrities. I am surely not one of them. Like my dad, I was a storyteller, who could fascinate his friends with tales of his life experiences. People often said to me over the years that I should write down the stories I was telling. Here they are.

I decided to call this story *Not Really Hollywood* because the story is not about Hollywood, but is rather about a young boy growing up behind the scenes as the Real Beaver and his experiences over the course of much of his adult life.

Joe Connelly and Bob Mosher were a team that produced much more than the Beaver show. Their incredible talent has given countless viewers more than eight decades of viewing pleasure. Beginning in the 1940s with "Amos and Andy," they have been involved in over twenty-three movies, radio, and television shows. Their greatness has inspired other producers to reboot additional movies and television shows. One click on the television in 2020 gives viewers access to family comedy that people of all ages can watch.

Leave It to Beaver featured such characters as Beaver, Wally, Lumpy, Whitey, Richard Rickover and of course the icon, Eddie Haskell. All were created from true experiences of our family and friends. A one-time family episode or comment would often make it into the show.

My dad once told me you can have a great product or a bad product, but if you don't have a plan to market all your work, it will become a loser. Connelly and Mosher were focused not only on producing and writing, but also on marketing their artistic products. They used books, comic books, a board game, a pinball machine, lunch pails, and trading cards to market their work. Today collectors can find t-shirts, dolls, cars, photos, and clocks associated with their shows. As for the gamblers, they can deposit their cash into a Munster slot machine.

The reality of my dad's philosophy has guided me through my life experiences. My early years were spent growing up in a semi-dream world in Bel-Air. Then,

I spent years pumping gas and caddying for executives and celebrities. Early in my business career, I chased down bench crooks and spit upholstery tacks. Next came the creation of a family life, as I became a parent of two fantastic children, along with my wife, a school principal. My dad's influence continued to guide me through the corporate world as I became a business consultant and a writer.

Not Really Hollywood
1. It's A Small World

It all began in Bel-Air, California, at a lovely white house on Ledo Way that stood on a mountain inside the West Gate of Bel-Air. At the time, I had an older brother and sister and one younger sister. Bel-Air was a home to all the Hollywood big shots of the time. My mom and dad, Joe Connelly, had moved there when I was about three years old. We had moved from a house in North Hollywood.

My dad was moving up in the Hollywood scene. The story of his success began in New York when he left the Walter Thompson Advertising Agency to work for Charlie Correll and Freeman Gosden, the voices and creators of the popular radio show "Amos 'n'Andy." The show first aired in 1928 and continued into the early sixties. The show had started back in New York. My mom was a New York girl and went to Marymount on the east coast. My parents were married in New York and moved to California when Correll and Gosden relocated to the west coast.

Bob Mosher and my dad became lead writers for "Amos 'n' Andy" in the late thirties. The writers created daily radio shows until 1943. "Amos 'n' Andy" then went to a weekly radio show until 1960. They wrote more than 1,500 shows.

One of my earliest memories was watching my dad and Mosher write a radio show. My dad would walk around and start to tell a story in the characters' voices. Mosher would be typing away with a cigarette hanging from his mouth. He would then stop typing and would speak up, adding a one-liner. This creative process that I was witnessing would become the foundation of their successes as premier writers, creators, and producers over the next four decades.

Later, in the early 1950s, my dad and Mosher would write shows for the television series *Amos 'n' Andy*. The show would air from 1951 to 1953. The show was later syndicated from 1954 into the sixties.

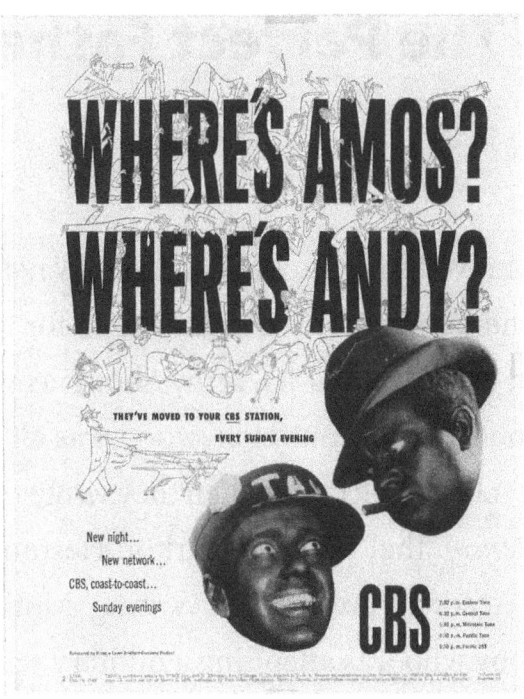

I would get home from school to watch the shows right before *Divorce Court*. Many years later, at the Monterey Peninsula Country Club in Pebble Beach, I recognized the Judge at the bar. We had a splendid time talking about the Golden Age of TV.

2. The Perfect Father

By the time we had moved into the Bel-Air Ledo Way house, my dad's career was moving forward, and he was writing radio shows for the likes of Phil Harris and "The Edgar Bergen and Charlie McCarthy Show," as well as doing freelance work for other Hollywood comics. But Hollywood was all about movies and the beginning of television. A big break came when they wrote the movie script for *The Private War of Major Benson* that starred Charlton Heston. My dad and Mosher were nominated for an Academy Award for "Writing, Motion Picture Story." The story was about a little boy who was attending a military school. My older brother at the time was attending a military school, so it may have made sense to my dad to write a story on this topic. Also nominated in that category was *Rebel Without a Cause,* starring James Dean. The winner was *Love Me or Leave Me*, starring Doris Day and James Cagney.

My first introduction to Hollywood came when my dad took Richard Correll, Charlie Correll's son, and I to Disney Studios on a Saturday to meet Walt Disney. Mr. Disney showed us how cartoons were created and the fascinating work that a cartoonist did by developing each image for every motion and the overlays. Richard and I were very popular when we arrived at Marymount Junior School in West Los Angeles the next Monday with all the treasures that Mr. Disney had given us.

Marymount was considered an all-girls school, but they allowed boys up to the third grade. While each class was composed mostly of girls, there were a handful of boys who would become the characters for the upcoming television series *Leave It to Beaver*, and my older brother and I would become the focus characters of the show.

My first crush was on a girl at Marymount. I was selected to dress up as Peter Pan and escort girls down the runway at a fashion show. My mom thought the scene would be darling. I ended up escorting my first love, Kristin Harmon, down the runway. Kristin's father was famous football player "98," who won the Heisman Trophy. A grade lower at Marymount was Kristin's brother, Mark, the star of the *NCIS* (Naval Criminal Investigative Service) television series. Sixty years after walking Kristin down the aisle, I was having dinner with Mark Harmon and mentioned that I had a crush on his sister. He replied, "Everyone had a crush on her." I proudly exclaimed, "But I was one of the first—in third grade!" Kristin later married Ricky Nelson.

My dad had been a strong track runner in high school. His running mate's nickname on the team was Beaver. Now a parent at Marymount, a girl's school, my dad would get the boys interested in sports. Dad was a big UCLA football fan. Red Sanders was the football coach at UCLA at the time, so my dad took us to meet the coach, and the boys and I ended up in the newspaper. A couple of boys in the photo would become the inspiration for Beaver's friends on the show. Second to the right is Richard, the son of Charlie Correll, who played Richie on *Leave It to Beaver*.

Red Sanders, UCLA football coach, fits shoulder pads on Terry Fotre while other Marymount Junior School boys look on. Clockwise, left to right, are Timothy Goger, Richard Connelly, Paul Kemnitzer, Donnell Doyle, John Ryde, Michael French (peeking around Coach Sanders' shoulder), John French, Stephen Merrin, Richard Correll, and Walter Osborne. The Marymount boys visited with the Bruin coach while on a field trip to the Westwood campus.

One of our favorite places to go after school or swimming practice was a place in Brentwood. In those days, there were no supermarkets—just small grocery stores. While our butler was getting groceries, we would go into the ice cream parlor next door. There was always a guy sitting at a table with his back to the wall. Sometimes he would say, "Give those kids free ice cream today." He was the owner of the place, and we thought he was a really cool guy. His name was Mickey Cohen, the notorious gangster. I sure am glad that we thanked him every time!

By this time, the Connelly family had grown. I was six or seven years old, and in addition to my older brother and sister and my younger sister, I had another brother. We were five, with more to come. My dad never forgave my younger sister for being born on January 1st, because he had to miss the Rose Bowl game.

To add to the confusion inherent in a house full of kids, we had a live-in cook, a nanny, and a butler. The Bel-Air house was under construction to add more rooms. In the end, the garage became a bedroom. We added on a new garage, built with stiles on the side of a mountain, and the patio became a projector room with an additional bedroom. I have little memory of my younger sister and brother because my dad wanted me to become a swimmer. So off I went to Brentwood Swim School for daily practices with my older sister.

Somehow my dad came up with the idea that I should swim the breaststroke completely underwater at a swim meet, which was allowed in those days. So at age six, I submarined myself for 25 yards and won a bronze medal. From that moment on, swimming became a way of life for me, up to the age of seventeen.

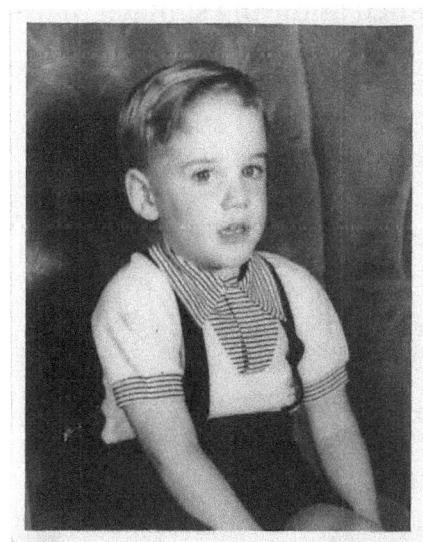

My dad would take us to all Amateur Athletic Union (AAU) meets from Santa Monica to Long Beach to Las Vegas. Las Vegas held an annual large swim event that my sister and I would attend with my mom and dad and my mom's mother. In those days, there were few hotels, and we always stayed at Sands. There was always an event. One year, we were kicked out of rooms because Elvis needed our suite. Ironically, my dad would later produce his last movie.

The best Sands experience was going to a Sammy Davis, Jr., show. Of course, my dad had the best booth in the house. When Mr. Davis would come out onto the stage, he would look up at our booth and announce that kids were there that night. In those days, entertainers did two shows a night. He would begin by singing and would then introduce May Britt and her parents from Sweden, who had just arrived in the United States. He would then go on dancing, singing, and playing every instrument in the band. One time, a two-hour show went on for over three and a half hours. As we were leaving, the people in line could not understand why they had had to wait so long. Mr. Davis commented in a book that it had been his best performance of all.

Living on a hill in Bel-Air, I grew up largely in seclusion because there were not many kids around. One of the hiccups that I recall along the way had to do with living on a Bel-Air hill with a pool surrounded by ivy. I just so happened to be prone to poison ivy. Due to the endless hours I spent swimming and my constant exposure to the plants surrounding our poolside play ground, I grew up with chlorine eyes and calamine lotion skin.

I always considered academics to be a hassle, and my vocabulary was not always the best. My words never seemed to come out right with my dad, and he was often amused by this. My older brother would never cease to point out that I did a lot of dumb stuff such as hiding spinach in my socks, being dared to climb a tree and getting stuck, faking baths, giving the house painter booze, and the embarrassment of short pants, which I will explain shortly. Zipping my pants may have been a problem.

NOT REALLY HOLLYWOOD

We would rent a house every summer on Lido Island or stay at the Balboa Bay Club in Newport Beach, California. Due to the size of our family, some of us stayed at the house and others, at the club. The only thing that separated us was Newport Bay.

3. Beaver's Short Pants

Because of my grades in school, one summer I had to attend summer school. In Orange County, there was a military school where they filmed the movie *The Private War of Major Benson*. My mom's grandmother was taking care of us, and on the first day of school, she tried to send me off in short pants. The problem was that even in the summer, you just do not wear short pants to a military school. Grandmother did not understand this. After a great deal of crying and yelling, I went off to school in short pants. The day did not go so well, and I was the laughingstock of the school. The next day started with the same routine, except that my dad had returned. My dad, not wanting to contradict my mom's mother, said that I had to wear short pants. In the garage, however, he had stashed a pair of long pants for me to wear. This scene went on throughout the summer. Years later, it would become one of my favorite episodes of *Leave It to Beaver*.

Living on a hill in Bel-Air was a disadvantage in terms of seeing my friends. Everything had to be scheduled. I typically only saw my friends when there were birthday parties. Kids' birthdays in Hollywood were always grand events. Once I was invited to Richard Correll's birthday, and my mom purchased a giant stuffed rabbit as a gift. Of course, I had a tantrum over it, crying that I could not take a gift like this to my friend's party. I solved the problem by snatching a camera from our house and giving it to Richard instead of the rabbit. That night, Richard's mom called us to investigate why I would give Richard an expensive camera with film in it. Well, that turned out to be another one of my favorite *Leave It to Beaver* shows.

Swimming took up a great deal of my time. By third grade, my parents had shipped me off to St. John's Military School, about an hour away from home (there were no freeways in those days). My older brother and I took the drive every day. I wanted to join my brother at St. John's because they had a swim team and their coach was the same one I had worked with in Brentwood. The school was just like the one in the movie *The Private War of Major Benson*. In fact, St. John's was the original choice of location for shooting the movie, but the school declined. St. John's was complete with Stars and Stripes uniforms, the ranks, a commander, and catholic nuns with their rulers.

My brother was a big football star for the school. So as a third grader, I had to go out for the "C" football team. As I came out of the locker room with the full gear, I looked like the Beaver in the new *Leave It to Beaver* movie. Even the 5th graders feared me due to my brother's playing ability. After one practice, I was demoted to the 3rd string. None of my friends from Marymount ventured to the school, so for me school was a whole new experience of meeting kids who lived many miles away. The bright side was that I always had my brother to protect me from the bullies.

Every year, there was a big football homecoming weekend. My brother being the star player meant the whole family would attend. We were all having breakfast one homecoming morning at our spacious dining room table. Halfway through our meal, my mom mentioned that it was time to go. My dad said not until we finish eating. We thought our parents were talking about the football game, but we later learned that the reason for needing to depart was much more important than any sporting event: during the game, I found out that I had another sister! I didn't even know that my mom was pregnant.

Military school was quite different from Marymount. Besides the military uniform, we had to salute our ranking officers, the nuns were a lot meaner, and we received weekend detentions for just about anything. We earned demerits for being late for school or classes, not saluting an officer, messing up in marching drills, and having a less-than-perfect uniform tie or shirt. Detention became my worst fear. To make matters worse, if we talked during class, we had to endure the nun's ruler across our knuckles in addition to receiving demerits.

Unfortunately, the swimming was not much fun either. The varsity team was made up of 7th and 8th graders, and they did not like a 3rd grader competing and out-swimming them. Military school was all about winning: on the sports field, in parade marching, in the classroom.

There was a swim meet in which all the military schools participated. Before the meet, there was a big trial event to see what team you were going to be on. When I finished, I had made the varsity team, but upper classmates said that I had cheated with my fast starts off the blocks and my flip turns. The coach moved me down to junior varsity for 5th and 6th graders. The varsity team finished dead last in an important meet at Black-Foxe Military Institute. Junior varsity, on the other hand, finished first. I had won every single event. The coach sent me in to the commander with a trophy that was almost bigger than I was.

Only a few African American kids attended my school. Every year, the school had a large carnival. My mom brought me there one year to enjoy the festivities. Because my mom loved to live in the sun, she had a deep tan. One day at the carnival, she was approached by the mother of an African American student. Thinking that my mom was a member of the African American community, the woman mentioned to her that there were very few African American students at the school. My mom was a sweetheart and avoided confrontation at all costs, so I think she just smiled at the comment. Moments later, when I suddenly ran up and asked my mom for a dollar, the woman looked shocked to see a freckle-faced, blond child. Her son would later become my friend.

The boy's dad owned a mortuary, and I would spend time at their Sherwood Lake house with the family. I found out later in life that, sadly, my friend's family had experienced racial hostility from residents of the community simply because they owned a home at this exclusive lake. To me, the family was the exact same color as my mom. I knew nothing about race, only friends.

Starting my second year at St. John's was a disaster. My older brother had graduated and was not there to protect me. The older boys with their high ranks were out to get me because my brother was gone. The demerits I received for seemingly nothing were adding up, and detention became a way of life on the weekends.

The final issue I faced at St. John's occurred when I had to go to detention on a Saturday for the entire day. If you were late, you had to kneel for half the day. One thing the Connelly family was not was punctual, even with a maid, a butler, and a nanny. At the time, there were six of us kids, so there was always a lot going on, not to mention the long drive to school. When I knew I was going to be late, I would throw a tantrum (I threw many in those days) and would find a place to hide. That particular tantrum turned out to be the grand finale that thankfully ended my military career.

By the middle of 4th grade, I was attending my fourth grammar school. Luckily, this time, my school was just up the street from our Bel-Air home.

The proximity of the school gave me more time for my daily swim at the club. At that point, I was doing well in my AAU age group. My one disadvantage: very small feet.

All great swimmers had large feet that acted like flippers. So my dad put me on a weight program—perhaps the first for a swimmer. I had to do a half hour of each stroke holding two two-pound weights each day standing in my parents' master bedroom, rather than in the pool.

My dad was the one who would take us to all the swim meets on the weekends. At one event at the Los Angeles Coliseum Olympic pool, he saw a diver and commented, "That's my Wally." The future *Leave It to Beaver* star.

4. Cat Out of the Bag

My dad and Mosher were working on a new television show when I was in sixth grade. The pilot, called "It's A Small World," debuted in 1957. The half-hour pilot was a success, and a new series began. There were some major changes to be made, however. The new show was called *Leave It to Beaver*. Hugh Beaumont replaced Casey Adams as Beaver's father, and Tony Dow replaced Paul Sullivan as Beaver's brother.

By 1958, *Leave It to Beaver* had become a weekly series. I had no idea that I was the inspiration for the show, until a certain trip to New York. Every year, after the end of the season, my mom, dad and I, along with the cast, took a trip to the east coast to meet with reporters and advertisers. As I mentioned, our family was not punctual. We made our flight just in the nick of time. When we arrived in New York, a man came on the airplane and asked, "Did anyone leave their red station wagon at the curb of the airport with the car running?" Yes, it was us.

The trip included my dad, mom, Jerry Mathers, and Tony Dow. Jerry "The Beaver" and I got along well. In fact, Jerry was just two days older than I was. Tony was like my big brother and was always bugging me.

Our realization that the show was a hit happened at the New York Zoo. As we walked through the zoo, kids started yelling, "It's the Beaver!" A crowd formed around the two young boys. From that moment on, they were true TV stars.

Later on that trip, we were at an orphanage sponsored by an advertiser in Iowa. After lunch, the kids surrounded Jerry and Tony, and they had to be placed on an old flatbed truck for safety. The kids and reporters were shouting out questions to the stars on the truck, and there was a group of young girls around my dad. He asked the girls if they wanted to meet the real "Beav." As I signed my first autographs, I realized that the show was about me.

5. Boat Builders

While in New York, my dad and I would spend one day driving down to New Jersey to spend some time with relatives. I believe my dad was the nephew of the two sisters who lived together. The reason for the trip was not really to socialize, but rather to explore the aunts' Civil War memorabilia.

Near the end of the night, they would start giving my dad some of the items, such as guns, swords, and photos. Our house was full of these artifacts. One of them that I recall, in particular, looked like a crafted gun box. When we got into our limousine, we opened the old container, which happened to be full of bottles. I made the mistake of opening one of the bottles. That limo would never be the same again. The bottle I had liberated was booze that had not been opened since the Civil War.

Life in the Bel-Air house with so many people around was interesting, to say least. We had three live-in employees, plus six kids, my mom, and my dad. My father spent time with us at swim meets, at football games on weekends, and during the summer. From an early age through to my late teenage years, our family would spend a good deal of the summer in Newport Beach. We were members of the Balboa Bay Club and stayed either in Apartment 514 or in a house on Lido Island.

My dad was a merchant mariner, and one summer he purchased me a dinghy sailboat. We launched it in front of Balboa Bay Club. Not fifteen feet from the beach, my dad yelled, "Hardalee!"- a sailing term meaning to move the sail to the boat's protected side. Then the dinghy suddenly flipped over, and we found ourselves in the water with a laughing audience on the beach.

After a few years, my dad upgraded the dinghy sailboat to a Lido 14. We named it KARI, a combination of my sister's name, Karen, and mine. We got the idea of combining our names from the name of my dad's production company, which was called Kayro, named after the wives, my mom Katie and Mosher's wife, Rose.

In those days, the Hollywood crowd would take an occasional trip to Ojai Inn. The only problem with these trips was that they were lengthy because we had no freeways. Sepulveda Boulevard and Ventura Boulevard were our highways. The Inn was a favorite getaway for celebrities

such as Clark Gable, Lana Turner, and Ronald Reagan. It was beneficial for my dad to network with Hollywood executives and celebrities.

Ronald Reagan was a good friend of the family. He was an actor and president of the Screen Actors Guild (he served six terms). Later, in 1957, he would be the host of the pilot of *Leave It to Beaver* on the General Electric Theater sponsored by MCA. Who would have known then that my dad's good friend would become the governor of California and then president of the United States?

6. Most Interesting Characters

My mom was a character. Much like someone named June from a TV show, my mom always wore a dress, high heels, and pearls. She would go to Catholic mass every day and then to her friends' houses to watch them play bridge. On sunny days, she would be out on the patio soaking up the sun.

At parties, Alfred Hitchcock, who was fascinated with my mom, would spend hours just talking to her. Hopefully, the idea for the Bates Motel did not come from any of those conversations. Hitchcock's movies were very prominent at Universal Studios at the time. I remember meeting him a few times on sets.

My mom was always there to drive us places and go to our swim practices. Once when she had me and my older sister in the car, she was yelling at the two of us to stop fighting in the back seat. To keep us quiet, she took command. She pulled over at a bus stop and told an elderly lady that she would take her anywhere she wanted to go. As we drove down Sunset Boulevard, there was not a sound from me or my sister. That was my mother's way of fixing situations.

Thanksgivings were always a magnificent event for our family. We had a dog named Mike; he was famous for crushing through screen doors to get into the house. One year, we got a call from Ray Milland, the actor, who lived on an adjacent hill. He called to inform us that our dog had stolen his turkey. Luckily, my dad had produced his television show. My dad told Ray he could have one of our turkeys. The only problem was that Mike had also stolen one of our turkeys. The following Monday, Mike was nowhere to be found. My mom reported that Mike had been sent to a "farm."

For another Thanksgiving, my dad and his partner had decided to raise two turkeys and eat them for the holiday feast. We became very fond of those turkeys growing up in our backyard. Then came the day for the kill. With hatchet in hand, my dad and his partner went outside to take care of the matter. Feathers flying, the kids were instructed to go inside. I never found out whether our families had eaten those turkeys for dinner, but I do know that I myself did not eat turkey that year.

I hated eating at the dining room table because my parents always made me clean my plate. I disliked vegetables, especially spinach. I would hide the spinach in my sock and put it in a drawer in my room. About a week later, my parents would find it. That tradition inspired yet another *Leave It to Beaver* episode.

Of all my siblings, I was the kid who most often got picked on at the table. One night, I had had enough. I threw my tantrum and started up the stairs. Midway, I turned to my dad and indignantly proclaimed, "I am not going to give you any more lines for your TV shows!"

For over fifty years now, every time I watch the show, I discover a new aspect of an episode that was inspired by one of my antics.

Some of the episodes I have not yet mentioned are actually my favorites.

Beaver Takes a Bath. My dad told me to take a bath before dinner. During dinner, water drops mysteriously began dripping onto the dining room table. Yes, I had forgotten to turn off the bath water.

Beaver and Andy. A painter was painting our house. He asked me for some of my dad's stuff. Well, he ended up as drunk as a skunk.

Beaver in the Soup. I was at a friend's house, and he dared me to climb a tree. The slight problem with this idea was that I could not get down. Thankfully, the fire department saved the day.

Beaver Takes a Walk. Like most dads, mine would often tell us how he would walk to school ten miles in the snow.

Beaver Takes a Drive. I needed to move my mom's large red station wagon out of the garage. So I put it in neutral and started to push it back. Well, it conveniently rolled across the street and blocked the road so that no one could pass. Of course, it took me half an hour to find the keys.

Beaver's Jacket. A classmate of mine left his jacket at our house. I forgot to bring it to school the next day, which developed into my first fight.

Beaver's Prep School. My parents sent me off to a prep school in Washington, D.C. Really, me as a preppy!

Merchant Mariner. My dad was a Merchant Mariner in the late 1930s. Not much help with my dinghy lessons.

Wally's Haircomb. My older brother was always making an Elvis statement.

Uncle Billy. My dad had a friend who sometimes watched me and told me endless stories of his implausible feats. Even I knew that no one person could have done what he claimed to have accomplished.

Mistaken Identity. When I was around Richard Correll, I was always doing something mischievous and getting in trouble. In one episode, Richard got in trouble for impersonating the Beaver to the cops.

Dad at times had arguments with TV censors over some of the shows. Dad usually won. Watching reruns of the "Beaver" show, viewers may notice some classic comical lines. Probably the most famous, and what I consider to be the second best line of all-time, was June's request: "Please be easy on the Beaver tonight."

All my dad's TV shows had those quick lines. I once asked my dad how they would come up with them. His reply was, "Twelve-year-old Grant's Scotch." By the way, what I consider to be the very best line of all-time came from *The Newlywed*

Game, when Bob Eubanks, the host, asked where was the best place the couple had had sex. One wife's reply was, "When he nipped me in the butt, Bob."

Another great line from *Leave It to Beaver* is from an episode where Ward was balancing the checkbook. He had difficulty finding an eight-dollar check. He asked June about it. She commented that she could not find it, so she wrote an eight-dollar check and tore it up. Ward replied, "You should be in Washington." That was in the sixties!

7. Beaver's Freckles

The school up the street did not last long. Soon, I was back to a Catholic school and the nuns. I started my fifth grammar school at St. Paul's in West Los Angeles. I was now entering fifth grade.

The good news: I had a ride every morning because the church that my mother went to each day was connected to the school. The bad news: the mass that she attended was an hour before class started. Once again, I faced the challenges of starting a new school and making new friends who lived miles away from our Bel-Air house.

My dad was a big shot at St. Paul's because they were building a new church, and my dad had donated an altar. Being Catholic was of great importance to my dad, and he would attend many religious events. The cardinal of Los Angeles would sometimes come to Bel-Air and have mass at our house. My dad received all kinds of awards and plaques from the church. I imagine that he must have been spending big bucks.

While other kids from St. Paul's were playing flag football, basketball and baseball, I was dedicated to swimming. My dad was a big sports fan, and I loved all sports. He would take me to all the UCLA and Notre Dame games and, in fact, being Irish, he took me back to South Bend for football games. When the Dodgers moved to Los Angeles, my dad had a good friend who headed the marketing team that had brought the Dodgers west. Everything my dad did was a production. I was picked up at the house and had dinner with the Dodgers' General Man-

ager, Buzzie Bavasi, and then was off to the Coliseum for a Los Angeles Dodgers vs. Milwaukee Braves game (Yes, the Braves played in Milwaukee in 1958). I sat by myself behind home plate and met celebrities such as Hank Aaron and other Hall of Fame players. I even had my picture taken with Leo Durocher.

The Dodgers were pitching a lesser-known player named Sandy Koufax against Lew Burdette. Around the 7th inning, I was taken up to the broadcast booth to sit with Vin Scully and Gerry Doggett. The Dodgers lost 2 to 1 that night on a Burdette home run over "Moon Shot" screen.

Many years later, when I caddied at Bel-Air for Scully, I mentioned that I had met him years ago at the game. He looked at me and said, "You had a lot more freckles then." What a memory! I had thrown away my black-and-white photo with Durocher because my freckles stood out so boldly in the photo. There was a Beaver show all about freckles.

My dad and I were always traveling to New York on his business trips. On one occasion, we were having dinner at the 21 Club with the owner of the Los Angeles Rams, Dan Reeves. The Rams were a really bad team in those days. It was late in the evening and after a good many drinks, Mr. Reeves decided to show me how the Rams players should block. Reorganizing the 21 Club by moving chairs around, he made a pathway to demonstrate. Management was not thrilled, but they decided to accept this behavior in exchange for witnessing insider information on blocking techniques. With waiters and me as the defensive line, Mr. Reeves showed us the moves. After the demonstration, he decided that we should fly back to Los Angeles to watch a game that weekend on the field. Unfortunately, the Rams failed to block, and lost.

My dad was a UCLA fan. We would go to all the home games. Our tickets were always on the forty-yard line in the parents' section. Every Thursday night, big UCLA linemen would show up at our house, and a few dollars would change hands. For the UCLA/USC games, our chauffeur would take us to Wilshire Country Club, where we would have brunch and ride the bus to the game. The only problem was that the bus was loaded with USC fans in their cardinal and gold, while we were in our baby blue. The USC fans sang the fight song through the entire bus ride. That sparked my longtime hatred for USC and horses, and, yes, any team that beats USC is my favorite team to this day.

The football games with my dad were fantastic. My mom, on the other hand, had me going to cotillion dance classes every weekend at the Bel-Air Hotel. Of course, none of my playmates from Marymount was ever stuck going to these classes, only a girl from St. Paul's the Apostle School. The boys  always made jokes that I was taking a girls' class. Naturally, my dad wrote a *Leave It to Beaver* show on the subject.

My mom was always trying to fix me up with dates. One rainy UCLA/USC game, it was all set. My date was my dance partner from class. The boys were always making fun of her at school, even though she was very pretty (or perhaps precisely for that reason). She handled the rainy conditions with style, but dumped me for a much older boy who was sitting next to us at the game. I really did

not mind because I was focused on the game, but I guess the experience of being dumped there deepened my hatred for USC.

My dad attempted to add to my schedule the one major sport that was missing from our lives: basketball. Jerry West of the Lakers would have a basketball camp during the off-season. Mr. West showed up at the Bel-Air house one day to pitch his camp to us. The only problem was that he hit his head on the ceiling of the house. He gave me some pointers, but the camp never happened. Swimming was my sport at the time.

The swim school in West Los Angeles was not stocked with the best swimmers, so we decided to try a new swim club in the San Fernando Valley. Unfortunately, it was about an hour away (still no freeway). We would practice every weeknight, and then go to swim meets on the weekends. Thankfully, my older sister came along, too. In most cases, the butler would drive us over the mountain, and my dad would pick us up. But there were times when we had to take a cab home because my dad would forget to pick us up. My weekday schedule meant being to school by 7 a.m., at swim practice from 4 p.m. to 6 p.m., and back to Bel-Air around 7 p.m. There was not much time for me to make friends or do my homework.

8. Eddie's Double Cross

By 1959, *Leave It to Beaver* was being renewed each year. On occasion, I would go to the studio and watch the filming, but my main contact with the cast members of the show occurred during our trips to the east coast. By this point, my parents had seven of us and had remodeled the house three times. My older brother had his driver's license, and the trouble had begun. There were gangs in West Los Angeles at the time. The best way to explain the gangs is to say that they were similar to the ones in the movie *West Side Story*. The gang members had their jackets with large logos on the back.

My brother shared a room with me, and he had a friend who would always pick on me. As I would later comment in interviews, "He was a lot meaner than Eddie Haskell." My dad told me that Ken Osmond, who played Eddie, "was the best child actor because his real-life personality was the opposite" of the personality he played on the show.

My brother and his friend would tell me about the gang fights, and at times would show me their switchblades. To pass the time at the house, I would play baseball off the wall in the front yard. Once while I was busy playing out front, a car pulled up, and two men in suits came up and flashed their police badges. They asked if I knew where Joseph Connelly was. Thinking that they were talking about my dad, I responded that he was at the studio. They shouted, "Not your dad! Your brother." I really thought I would be going off to jail for giving false information.

My dad would not let my older brother drive me around much, probably for two very good reasons: the gangs and his driving record. One time, I was allowed to go to Disneyland with the son of one of my dad's friends, Fred MacMurray.

Fred MacMurray was a Disney star and one of the wealthiest actors in Hollywood. Mr. MacMurray told his son that the tickets would be at will call. When we arrived at will call, we found out that we had to pay for tickets. MacMurray was known to be frugal, but we never thought that he would have been that cheap.

Luckily for me, we had been going to that magical place for many years. When in Newport Beach, the family would take a ride to Disneyland. On my birthday, my dad would take me and a group of boys to stay the night at the Disneyland Hotel. He would reserve a suite, and each of my friends would have their own room. Two days would give us almost enough time to go on all the rides with our book of tickets from A to E, but E-tickets were for the premium rides.

Around that time, my older brother was doing his best to keep up with the times and the styles. His haircut was a duplicate of Elvis or Conrad Twitty, and sounds of "Jailhouse Rock" blasted throughout our house. My brother's guitar playing and singing were awful, but the song was extremely fitting for him.

My older sister also got into music in the late 1950s. She took piano lessons. To this day, I remember the only song that she could play, "The Camels are Coming."

For some reason, I always spent time with my older sister rather than my older brother, perhaps because he was always in trouble. We would take trips together across the pond to Europe. We swam together. We even had our tonsils out at the same time. As usual, my dad made the hospital stay into a huge production. Our hospital room had an adjoining suite for my parents to stay in. Having two of us in the hospital at the same time created a problem for me, though. When the doctor and nurse came in to give us shots, they started with my sister, which meant that I knew what was coming. I panicked every time. I tried everything under the sun to change their minds about where to give me the shots.

9. New Doctor

I had other problems, too. The hills surrounding our house developed into my worst nightmares. I had a fear of rattle snakes. I would dream they were attacking me and wrapping themselves around my body when I was swimming alone in the pool.

My life was not the life of a normal kid. All my old friends were going to a Catholic school in Beverly Hills, my older sister was entering high school, and the nanny was busy taking care of the young ones. With my mom attending mass every morning, I had to become an altar boy. That meant I had to learn some Latin, which was not good for a kid who could not even master the English language. I nearly got the whole procedure down pat, but the Latin language was just not my specialty. So at each mass, I ended up mumbling my way through it all.

The nuns at my Catholic school were nice, maybe because of who my parents were. Every May, my family would travel to Europe. My parents would take me out of class before the end of the year. I think the only reason I received passing grades was that upon my return from Italy, I would show the nuns my religious treasures that had been blessed by the Pope. I do not remember ever seeing a report card. I would just somehow move up to the next grade.

In later years, my wife interviewed for a teaching job at St. Paul's. When the principal asked if she was part of the Connelly family, she answered yes, and that she was married to Ricky. My wife asked how I had done in school, and only a nun could have come up with such a kind answer. To avoid saying "slow," she replied "self-pacing."

I was never in the inner circle with the boys at school due to my swimming and trips to Europe. In eighth grade, I did try out for the basketball team, but every time, the boys told the coach I was no good at the sport. The day of the final cut, I had a bicycle accident and missed the cut (even though I was good). By my senior year in high school, I was the most valuable player on the basketball team.

That bike accident meant going to see Dr. Blood, our family doctor, which had been a fear of mine since the age of four. In the 1950s, people did not go to the doctor's office; the doctor came to the patient's house. When my brothers or sisters were sick, my mom would give them some type of gift. So, naturally, I contrived an illness in hopes of receiving my own present. It only took one time for me to learn from that mistake.

Dr. Blood showed up, and the needle came out. Oh no. And yes, the ordeal became the subject of a *Leave It to Beaver* episode. Who would have thought there actually could have been a Beverly Hills family doctor by the name of Dr. Blood? A child's nightmare in the flesh!

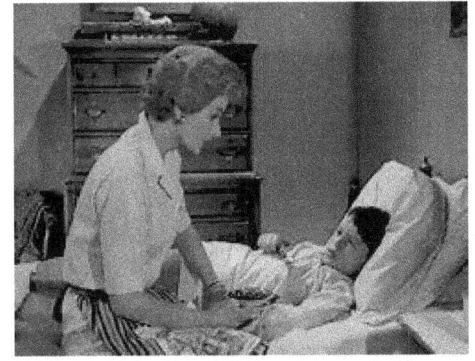

During that final year, 8th grade at St. Paul's, the Bel-Air fire occurred. We could see the smoke from school. My dad had left the studio midday and convinced an L.A. motorcycle police officer to give him a lift to the house. He told the officer that he had a gun collection that would create an explosion. When he arrived home, he stood on the roof wearing his Brooks Brothers suit to protect him from the flames. That night, my dad and I stood watch for as long as the fire was in sight. There were only four houses on our street, and two of them burned to the ground. All the nearby houses were also destroyed.

Richard Nixon had the same idea as my dad to attempt to save his Bel-Air home. They both saved their houses in the 1961 fire. In the 1960 election, some prominent Hollywood executive had asked my dad to work on Nixon speeches. He needed to add some humor to them. Even though Nixon lost, he sent a letter of thanks to my dad.

The final chapter at St. Paul's was sports awards night. I was invited to go because of a CYO swim meet for all the Catholic schools in Los Angeles. My dad had come home late and told me that I had to wear a coat and tie. I told

him that none of the other boys would. After my tantrum, I did not go. Yet another Beaver show was born.

I made it to the finals of the CYO swim event at the coliseum. Our team finished second and received a big trophy. They gave me all the recognition because I was the only one from the school on the team.

The Bel-Air house would become my sports practice field. In the early years, it was my baseball field. Later, it became my driving range for golf. Home plate for baseball was in front of the living room. Those foul balls would take out a few window panes from time to time. Of course, I would not tell anyone and simply close the curtain. Much like in another *Leave It to Beaver* story.

Years later, I used our yards for golf practice. I would try to hit wedges over the house down toward the pool. A onetime miss hit took out a window pane in the master bedroom. That ended that golf lesson.

When I worked as a caddy, I would lighten the club members' bags by taking out their old, beat-up golf balls. So I started a collection. One fine day, a friend and I decided to hit them from the hill in the backyard. After a while, there was a knock on the front door. An angry man said someone had been hitting golf balls onto his roof. Luckily for me, my friend had been listening to the conversation and rushed back to the yard to hide the evidence. So we took the guy to the backyard, and he looked down at his house. He said, "Jack Nicklaus could not hit a ball that far." Obviously, he was not a golfer and had little knowledge of the launch angle for projecting a golf ball. I promptly mentioned that the balls could have been coming from a house on the other hill and sent him on his way.

10. Ward's Problem

Our trips to Europe were always an adventure. The first adventure was had by just my parents and my older sister and started before we even left the states. We needed to get passports; all went well except for my dad's passport. His birth certificate read "Boy Connelly," which created a two-week governmental debate and almost delayed the trip.

For my dad, it only got worse from there. We left Los Angeles flying first-class to New York, and that's when the trouble began. An Italian doctor, who was a friend of my dad's, encouraged him to fly coach across the Atlantic. He had explained that Alitalia flights were never full and that we would all have plenty of seats in the back to sleep three across. Well, the plane just happened to be full that day. As soon as we boarded, my dad started yelling. There were no first-class seats available, and the flight turned out to be a disaster. Upon our arrival in Rome, we were picked up by a chauffeur. When my dad gave him the name of our hotel, he gave us an astonished look. Yes, it was a real dump.

After Rome, we went to Paris. One night, we had dinner with Mr. George Allan Hancock, a multimillionaire, and his entourage. His fortune had come from the oil business, and he was known for donating the La Brea Tar Pits. Mr. Hancock and I had some things in common. He would swim every day in his indoor pool and was interested in my swimming. Also, when I told him about my early connections to Walt Disney, he told me that he had donated the trains to Disneyland.

The dinner was very interesting because we were the only group in the restaurant. His group included his wife, his accountant, and a fighter pilot from World War II. The accountant paid all the bills. The fighter pilot talked about his kills in the war. But most interesting of all was Mr. Hancock's wife. His son was supposed to be married in San Francisco when an earthquake hit. Due to the upcoming marriage, he had given his suite to his son. The suite was crushed during the earthquake, and his son had died. Mr. Hancock ended up marrying his son's fiancée.

My dad would give the commencement speeches at Hancock College in Santa Maria, California. Mr. Hancock did everything in style. He had my dad picked up by a helicopter, and they made a stop at Vandenberg Air Force Base to visit the missile cyclones. Mr. Hancock had donated the land. He even offered to help out my troubled brother by setting him up as a cattle rancher in Santa Maria. Of course, my brother declined.

At some point along the way, traveling to countries where languages other than English were spoken became a problem for me and a fear of mine. On one of our early trips to Paris, my dad and I went out one night in our rented car, and we witnessed violent student protests going on in Paris. We got lost while driving the back streets. My dad got out of the car to ask a police officer with a machine gun for directions. The next image I remember was the officer poking my dad with the barrel of the gun, pushing him back to the car. I had never seen my dad so nervous. The translation from English to French must have gone really badly. For this reason, I travel mostly to English-speaking countries.

One important lesson I learned from my parents was to adapt to any situation. Flying home on Alitalia was not an option as far as my dad was concerned. So for this trip, he decided to fly first to England and to stay at an MCA/Universal Studios Flat (apartment) with a full-time butler and maid. Then we were off to South Hampton to take the SS United States ocean liner home. The accommodations on the ship were not up to my dad's standards, due to our last-minute reservations. By my standards, though, it was a positive experience. The SS United States ocean liner was the fastest luxury liner in the world.

The first night out, the ship was really rocking and rolling. The dining room was empty, so I ate at the captain's table. At one point, the conversation turned to how I could handle the rough seas. I commented that I had been sailing since I was six-years-old and was a fish in water. I guess I had made an impression on the staff because throughout the rest of the trip, crew members gave me tours of the entire ship.

Our family continued to take cruises of this sort for years to come, and the groups we traveled with became increasing large. On one trip, we stayed in a villa in Italy. I was back in my element with the beach and water, but I did not appreciate what I considered to be the boring Vatican and museums. And I certainly was not a fan of eating food I did not recognize.

My other memories of that trip include delights such as my dad introducing me to beer and wine when we spent time together. Another is my first view of topless women. The beach had vendors that sold bikinis, and women would try them on right there on the sand. Much to my surprise, the Italian beach also had outdoor showers, where after a day in the sun and water, women would shower completely naked for all to behold. That trip ended with another sea voyage across the Atlantic. This time, we were on the SS Constitution and had a magnificent view of the Mediterranean and Rock of Gibraltar.

Each year, our entourage, which always included a catholic priest, would grow. On the last trip I went on with my dad, a Paulist priest traveled with us. He later became known as the Hollywood Priest. My dad helped produce a feature on him in a weekly television show called *Insight*. Their relationship had started at St. Paul's when my dad was working on the priest's weekly sermons for Sunday masses. Every Thursday night, the priest would come to the house, and he and my dad would prepare the sermon for Sunday.

Thursday nights happened to be the cook and the butler's day off. One night, my mother decided to cook instead of getting our regular meal from the Brown Derby. My mom seldom entered the kitchen, and did not even know how to turn the appliances on or off. Her specialty was burnt chicken, sometimes with the price tag still on. As for pasta, our real problems began when the Hollywood Priest remarked on how much he had enjoyed the meal. So every week, we ate the same old burnt meal. For fun, my sister and I would throw the pasta onto the kitchen ceiling to see just how overdone it was.

In the later years of the *Insight* show, I debuted in my one and only acting performance. I was a star football player who ended up in a hospital bed during a racial tension football game. I had no lines. I just played a beat-up kid.

My last trip to Italy with my family included that Hollywood Priest. He had logistical issues in Italy from the outset. He was 6'4" and the rental cars in Italy were extremely small. As we drove through the coastal mountains of Italy, my dad and he were in the front seat. My mom, sister, and I were packed like sardines in the back with no leg room whatsoever.

Father Hollywood was always an early riser. So every morning, I was awoken to rush off to serve as the altar boy at his masses, which was not a highlight of the trip at the time. As I look back on the experience now, however, I realize that it was quite an honor and privilege to serve at the Vatican.

The final straw for me on that trip occurred on the cruise back to the United States. I decided on the last morning that I was not going to serve mass. I was going to sleep in. My roommate, Father Hollywood, tried to wake me, but I was not about to move. So he summoned my dad, who promptly threw the cold water from the ice bucket on my head.

I immediately planned my payback. Father Hollywood did not like wine in his cup during mass. So as he tipped the cup, I poured the whole vessel of wine into it, and then a drop of water. He had to drink it all. A little while later, as he proceeded across the altar, he gave me a swift kick. With a smile, I repeated my efforts at the second pouring, and then received another swift kick. Besides my mother at the mass, there was a group of nuns. One nun commented to my mother, "The boys are not getting along today."

That was my last trip to Europe, and my third and final voyage across the Atlantic. Although my family would continue to travel to Europe every year, I would stay home

39

during their subsequent trips. All in all, my experiences had been extremely valuable, especially the Vatican tours, meeting Popes, seeing the smoke for a new Pope, servicing mass at the Vatican, visiting the museums, staying at fancy hotels, learning to play ping-pong on a wavy ship, and the sight of coming into New York harbor and of the Statue of Liberty. My other experiences had been a combination of good and bad: my introduction to booze, naked women, and bad hotels, not understanding what people were talking about, touring with priests, not spending time with friends, and, finally, a newfound interest in girls.

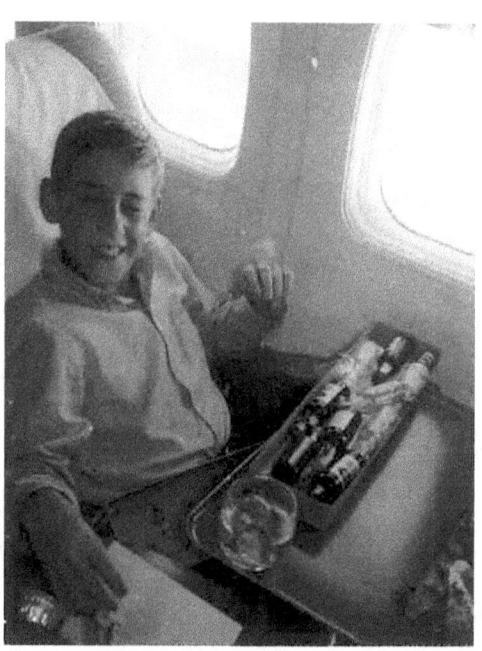

11. Boarding School

Becoming a teenager had some real advantages since my older sister had a car. That meant going to the other side of the hill for swim practices via her Falcon station wagon. By then, I had become a pretty good swimmer and was winning top events. The practices were always interesting because there were quite a few girls my age. The practice lasted for more than two hours, but we had our play time. The coach would demand that we all swim about a mile, or in swimming terms, 1,500 meters. He would start his watch and disappear across the street to a pizza restaurant. He would say he was going there to have pizza, but instead had a few drinks.

My two key events were the butterfly and individual medley, which was all four strokes: butterfly, backstroke, breaststroke, and freestyle. The problem with swimming at the public pool in the summer was that swimming lessons for kids and babies were offered there. That meant that they had to put a good deal of chlorine in the pool. After a long practice, my eyes would sting like crazy and be completely bloodshot. In those days, there were no goggles.

At the time, I had a sister who drove, and I had friends, both boys and girls, my age. My sister and I often had crazy ideas. I showed up at one practice with pink hair. One of my dad's TV advertisers was a hair color company. They sent samples to our house, and of course we had to try them.

That fall, I would be starting at Notre Dame High School in the valley. At the close of the summer, the coach would throw a party for the swimmers. During the party that year, all the girls were dancing. One of my favorites asked me if I could dance. She was hit with all my moves, thanks to all those dance lessons that I had not wanted to go to. I had some friends who were girls near the high school, so life was looking good as I was about to enter my new school.

Now after five grammar schools, one might have thought that I would have been promoted from eighth grade to ninth. But in Connelly tradition, there is always a snag, so let's add 5+1, the meaning of which will soon become apparent. All the boys from St. Paul's were heading to Loyola High, but that school had a poor swim team. Notre Dame High School would have been perfect. They had a great swim team with boys I had competed with for years.

My parents had other ideas for me, however. That summer, we took a trip to Washington, D.C. My parents had always hoped that I would become a priest, despite my being "self-pacing" and my inability to grasp the Latin language. My parents enrolled me in an east coast prep school in D.C. called Georgetown Prep. I should have known what the future would hold when, as a summer project, I was given three books to read and I had to complete book reports on all three. That fall, off I went to the east coast school, leaving all my friends behind yet again.

Talk about a fish out of water. The students at my new all-boy's school were the sons of elite scholars and political parents. Alumni past and future included Supreme Court justices, senators, congressmen, ambassadors, generals, Pulitzer Prize winners, NFL owners, the Kennedys, and the Shivers. The campus of Georgetown Prep was in Bethesda, Maryland, about a 30-minute drive from the White House. The campus was beautiful and had a 9-hole golf course surrounding the entire campus. I was the only west coast boy at the school, which was run by Jesuits. My first day was a shocker when my class assignment landed me in 8th grade and, of course, in a Latin class. By day's end, I had figured out how my dad had gotten me into the school: by holding me back a grade.

Georgetown Prep was the premier Catholic school. John F. Kennedy was president, and many of the kids at the school were the children of members of his administration. I never became very interested in politics, though. I had met President Ike because we would rent a house during the winter at Bermuda Dunes Country Club. Our house was just two doors away from his. Ike was an avid golfer, and some of the Nixon's would sometimes play with him. One of the houses that we rented was on the tenth hole about 200 yards out. When golfers would be off-target, their golf balls would splash into our pool. I would dive into the pool and retrieve their balls for a quarter. On one occasion, a bunch of secret service agents came charging up. When I asked for my fee, they were not happy. I'm not sure whose golf ball it was, but they were part of the Nixon clan, and no, I never got paid.

This self-pacing kid could not keep up with the super nerds at Georgetown Prep. My roommate was a cool kid whose dad was the president of Hertz International and whose older brother was also at the school. Winter came and with it, the first snow. The boys woke me up and kidded that this was my first time seeing snow. Of course, I denied it. But it really was a first for me.

There was a pond on the golf course that would freeze over. All the boys would go out on it to ice skate and play hockey. Something to note about boarding school is that to survive, you must accept pranks and be able to dish them out. Short-sheeting was popular. My first experience with this prank was thanks to our hall priest. Every school has that giant kid who looks as if he should be a senior but is really an eighth-grader. So he was a prime candidate for the sheet trick. We waited until he was at the pond to do the deed. Unfortunately, just as we had finalized the short-sheet, he suddenly showed up in a rotten mood. He looked at us and announced, "I fell into a hole on the ice," followed by, "What are you doing in my room?" That night at lights out, he found out. He chased me and my roommate all over the school. Thankfully, he was still thawing out and could not catch us.

The school was a football powerhouse in the D.C. area; the varsity team only lost one game in the two years that I was there. Due to the fact that I was not a scholar, the school expected me to play sports.

Living on the east coast exposed me for the first time to racism. Although the majority of the population in the D.C. area was African American, only one African American student attended Georgetown Prep. The upperclassmen would talk a lot about him. Additionally, when we would play football against African American teams and go to away games, the staff would discuss our exit plan with us. After the games, they instructed us to board buses for our security. With JFK as president, the civil rights movement was proceeding at full speed, so there was a good deal of tension.

With all of my free time on weekends, I started to take up photography. Georgetown had a darkroom in the basement, and I learned how to develop my own film. It came in pretty handy because I could stay on the football field or basketball court for the varsity games and take pictures for the yearbook.

One of the key reasons I was at the school was to swim. The story of my swimming at Georgetown Prep began when the 11th and 12th graders said an eighth-grader could not be on the varsity team. Georgetown had a world-class butterflyer at the time. My specialty stroke just happened to be butterfly. In a 100-yard race, I would always be a couple lengths behind him. In the final trials for the freestyle relay, the older boys told the coach that I was barely beaten at the wall for that event. Third grade history repeated itself. The coach recognized my ability and added me to the team. In high school, students could only swim in three events per meet. At our first meet, I finished second to our butterflyer and third in the medley (all the strokes in succession).

The last event was freestyle relay. Despite objections from the upperclassmen, I was the last swimmer in the relay. We were swimming against a school that we had never beaten in a dual match. Entering the final event, we were a few points behind and needed to win the event in order to win overall. I hit the water a few lengths behind, but I beat my opponent at the final wall. The whole team was in a frenzy, and I was the hero. The rest of the swim year was fantastic for me, and I became the first 8th grader ever to earn a varsity letter at the school.

4-man relay: Paul Fitzpatrick, Rick Connelly, Tony Peters, Greg Powell.

Life got a lot better after that. The school put up with my poor grades, and the head of discipline, a Jesuit priest, played fun pranks on us. A former AAU boxer, he really liked me, even when he would catch me in the midst of shenanigans like popping peas from a milk carton onto the ceiling of the mess hall. After a few detentions, I always returned to his good side.

During the spring, we often had barbeques, and the upper classes would be first in line. Touch football was big in those days because of the JFK clan playing every week. Father Discipline would tell me to go out for a pass against the upperclassmen. If I could catch it, I would be first in line and if I dropped it, last in line. It was great going first.

12. Beaver Sees America

I was lucky enough to be able to go home at Christmas to spend time with my family. I had no idea what my dad was doing. At Georgetown, we watched no television. *Leave It to Beaver* was near its end because Mathers was getting older, and they had to film from only one side due to his pimples. Being a swimmer had a real advantage in that I could surf at Huntington Beach and the Wedge. I spent the summer at swim practice in the San Fernando Valley and in Newport Beach with my family. Swim practice took place on the weekdays while my dad was at the studio. On weekends, we would drive down with him to Newport Beach. Of course, there were always a few AAU swim meets as well.

I still had the Lido 14 sailboat in Newport Beach. Dad always wanted me to participate in sailing races, but I was just no good at the sport. I liked tooling around the harbor and going places, though. At night, I would sail over to Balboa Island or the fun zone to meet with my friends.

My sailboat had no lights. On my trips back home, I would get caught by the harbor patrol, and I would have to be towed home. The nights with no wind were sublime.

One night, I met a girl my age named Kari (just like my sailboat KARI). My family had gone back to L.A., so I picked her up by sailing over to her parents' 65-foot yacht. I would sail on the edge by tipping the boat at an angle. Trying to impress Kari, I managed to flip the boat. One of the first things you learn in sailing is if you flip over, you take a cushion and place it on top of the mast. I forgot to do this, and the top of the mast hit bottom. The harbor patrol was out again!

It had been an enjoyable summer, but I would soon be back east with my swim trunks and a set of golf clubs to start playing on the school course.

Georgetown would not let me play football that next year because of my swimming. So during the season, it was back to photography and the dark room. Additionally, I would work out with the pre-season basketball players. I could have played with them, but their season was at the same time as the swim season, and the school would not let me do both.

I had a new roommate who was a genius. I think the school thought his intelligence would rub off on me. His father was in D.C. politics. Within a few months, however, my roommate was gone due to his father's going to jail during the Vice President Agnew fallout. The year was off to an excellent start, though. My friends and I could travel anywhere in D.C., and we were street-smart. We would find hiding places to smoke and read *Catcher in the Rye*. By this time, I could get around pretty well, thanks to my experiences taking buses, trains, and planes, and at times hitchhiking.

One day, I heard that my parents were in New York, so I hopped on a train to go see them. Richard Correll and his parents were staying at the same hotel to make a fun weekend of it. Also staying at the hotel were Richard Burton and Liz Taylor. They were big news due to their relationship, and Burton was performing *Hamlet*. My mom and dad were going to the play and had only two tickets. So my dad scalped a ticket, and my mom and I sat together. During the first act, there was a lot of buzz going on, and a lady sat next to me. In the past, I had seen a lot of great plays on Broadway, including *Bye Bye Birdie* and *Hello Dolly*, starring Carol Channing. *Hamlet* was not for me. After the first act, I turned to my mom and said, "This is boring. I am going back to the hotel."

In those days, the hotels had elevator operators. The next morning, we convinced the operator to call me and Richard Correll when she was going to pick up Richard and Liz. She picked us up, and we went up to the penthouse. The door opened, and they both entered. Liz was laughing. As we slowly dropped from floor to floor, Liz turned to Richard and said, "That is the boy who thinks you are boring." After a little small talk, the door opened at the lobby, where flashing light bulbs awaited the couple. A month later, I received autographed pictures of both of them.

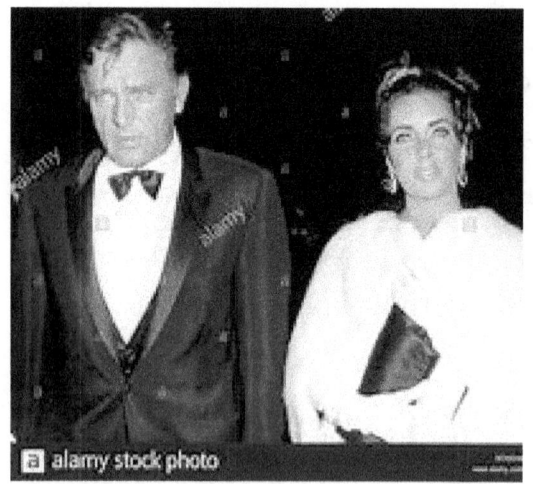

Richard Correll and I would spend some time together in the summer. We would have football games on their lawn, which had to be over100 yards, with other old friends. We began exploring other areas around Holmby Hills. There was one really large estate that looked like a house from *The Munsters*. We would climb the walls and head up to the estate that we deemed vacant. As we approached the house from the long curling drive, we heard the yelling of a caretaker, "Get out of here!" Over another fence, and we were in the woods. What we found next was a plush golf course. Richard decided that we could create havoc by letting golfers hit their shots onto the green and then running up and stealing the golf balls and running back into the woods. With golfers and caddies screaming at us, we did it a couple of times. What we had not figured out was that they would come to chase us. Fortunately, we found a manhole that was at least ten feet deep. From above, all we could hear from the players was, "We know that they were here. Where could they have disappeared to?" By the way, in later years, that old estate would become one of the most famous places of the Hollywood scene: the Playboy Mansion.

After our close call at that location, we tried other courses in the area. But this time, we scouted out our position before causing havoc for the golfers. We had to find a spot where the golfers would not see us. We knew that our plan had worked when we would hear the golfers pensively saying, "I know my drive landed in this area."

A golf course has just eighteen holes, so a golfer can only be fooled once. If you try it again, the next thing you know, you are being chased by a golfer wielding a club. Your getaway is jumping over a fence and onto an unknown estate. After being separated, we decided that the golf ball caper was not worth the risk.

That summer, I decided not to go to Europe with the family crew. My dad had his own "Tito," a flunky he called on to babysit me when I was alone in the Bel-Air house. Elmer was a real talker. He would start a story that was somewhat interesting, but you would never hear the ending because he would add more stories in between. We were told that he was ex-military and an old executive from General Motors in Michigan who had lost his job. He had had a rich wife who divorced him and lived in an apartment in Westwood. When my dad needed something, he was always there. He took all kinds of odd sales jobs, but his best job was at the bottle cap company. The company designed bottle caps that could have logos printed on them. They were intended to cap bottles after opening. Elmer would attend all of our parties, and his sales pitch would go on and on to all the guests. Every Hollywood celebrity in those days had their logo bottle tops. I am not sure if he sold any at our house, but we had hundreds of them.

That summer, Elmer would take me places such as to aircraft carriers and restaurants. While my family was in Europe, a strange development arose. A young Italian lady showed up at our house one day and took over one of our rooms. It turned out that my dad had hired a new nanny and sent her to our house while they were still traveling. She was good-looking and spent time at the pool when she had a chance. She would soak up the sun braless, and from the upstairs bedroom window, I would enjoy the show. At a certain point, Elmer caught me watching and ran down to ask her to put on her top. I never found out what happened to that lovely young lady, but Elmer really knew how to break up a good thing.

13. Beaver's Prep School

With summer over, it was back to D.C. The Beatles had performed across the pond, but I was really into folk music. My friends and I would go to record stores and change the prices of albums to a lower price. Until we got caught, that is. The head of discipline picked me up, and as he dropped me off, he told me to meet him in the basement in half an hour. I had seen him when he was mad and red-faced. I went to my room and put on five layers of clothing and headed downstairs. His first question was, "Who was with you?" I replied that I had done it myself. After he had smacked me around for ten minutes, he said, "You are not a snitch, but report to detention every day until I tell you otherwise." He told me he was going to call my dad but, to my knowledge, he never did.

At most schools, the students had to keep writing the same line over and over again. At Georgetown, we had to solve math problems as a consequence during detention. Everyone remembers the day of John F. Kennedy's assassination in Dallas. As much as I would like to avoid mixing tragedy and comedy, I must admit that I was in detention at the moment. When the news was announced, the school went into a complete shutdown. All the politicians' and diplomats' kids were gone. They had gone to the underground bunkers in the mountains in case of atomic war. As the whole country mourned, in D.C., there was an added element of fear. I attended the funeral march sitting in a tree on the route. The country had lost a president; our school had lost a Catholic and a community.

The swim season had started, and I had been ranked one of the best butterflyers on the east coast, even as a freshman. Just after Christmas, the school offered a ski trip. I decided to go and try the slopes for the first time. Unlike water and I, snow and I did not get along. On my last run, I fell and had a bone sticking through my pant leg. I was taken by ambulance to a Baltimore hospital. Upon my arrival at the hospital, the nurses said how much it was going to hurt when they took off my ski boot.

The nurses started by taking my information: where I lived and the occupation of my father. When I said Bel-Air, California, that sounded like it was continents away, but when I replied that my dad was a Hollywood producer, that hit a button. When I told them he created, produced, and wrote *Leave It to Beaver*, I was an instant star and started signing autographs.

Then a nurse told me they were going to put me under before removing the boot. The next thing I remember was waking up in a hospital room with a cast. As I left the hospital, doctors and nurses were signing my cast. I always told my dad it was great having a Hollywood big shot in the family.

"Sure, Rick, skiing's lots of fun."

Now, I was stuck on the east coast with a broken leg and no sports. Georgetown was not happy to have their swimming star out for the season. By spring, though, I started playing golf, and became one of the better freshmen golfers. Golf was advantageous as I did not have to sit in my room and study. By the end of the year, however, it was time for the school to ship me back permanently. So they gave me all C's and sent me packing.

14. Beaver's Cat Problem

Now that I was back in Southern California, the future looked promising. I started swimming practice and began driving school to get my license. I should have been swimming those miles in practice, however, rather than fooling around. Our coach would later train swimmers who went to the 1964 Olympics. At one large event, he entered me in a mile swim. The problem was that he had submitted the wrong time, and he had me down as breaking the world record at the time.

The coach would not tell the officials about the problem. The other swimmers in the event had a good deal of laughs during warm-ups and asked what I was going to do. As the public address system made the announcement of the swimmers, it was suddenly my turn: "Rick Connelly, Lane Five. If he matches his time, he will break the world record."

The key to the mile swim is pacing yourself at the start. When the gun sounded, I went out like a bat out of hell. I was leading by half of a pool length in the first 200 yards. I could hear and see the crowd roaring at each turn. After that, each 100 yards, more swimmers would pass me by. By the end of the race, they were lapping me. As I finished, I pulled myself out of the pool and acted as if I had a pulled hamstring. There was a moan from the crowd, and I had a good laugh with my competitors.

Soon after that meet, I would be turning sixteen, and that meant taking the driver's license test. One thing my siblings and I learned in the Connelly family was to share. We never knew what was going to happen at Christmas or on our birthdays. With seven of us, my mom would sometimes forget our birthday. On the other hand, one of us would sometimes receive a new car for our birthday. We learned to expect the unexpected. One Christmas, my mom forgot both my present and my older brother's gift. Someone had given my dad a cigarette lighter, so after she discovered that we had been missed, she said, "You two can share it." The only problem was I did not smoke.

The big event that year was that my older brother got married to one of my older sister's best friends from Marymount High School. She lived at the bottom of the hill from the Bel-Air house. She had a nickname: "The Cat Killer." One of my mom's best friends lived on the same street. My future sister-in-law had happened to run over their cat right in front of their house and, of course, kept driving.

So now my bad news older brother and the "cat killer" were getting married. Yes, it was a major Hollywood social event with the reception at Bel-Air Country Club. My dad's gift to the couple was one of the first Ford Mustangs. Plus my dad had given my older brother a job at Universal Studios as an editor.

Now that I had my license, I was sharing a station wagon with my sister. It did not take long for me to have my first altercation. A minor dent at a Jack-in-the-Box going less than five miles per hour turned into a major insurance fraud. The driver of the other car claimed that they had been injured and wanted money. Once they saw my Bel-Air address, they demanded dollars.

Some kids have "Wonder Years"; I had "crash years" for the next half a century. My nickname was "Crash Connelly Junior." The "junior" was due to my older brother's previous episodes. All told, there were a dozen crashes, some minor and a number of major ones that included cars such as a Rambler, Mustang, VW Van, and a Cortina, among others.

That summer was a good one; no more cabs over the hill for swim practice. Because I had been gone for two years, my friends were doing their own thing. The Bel-Air house was empty because the rest of the family was in Europe. At our house, we had a Bel-Air Patrol alarm button just inside the door that we would push to see if anyone would show up. I ended up really needing that button a few times for problems that arose.

My room was on the far side of the house surrounded by large glass windows. One night, I saw a man through my window. I crawled all the way to my dad's room. He had just come from a Friendly Sons of St. Patrick event. He grabbed his gun and went down the three flights of stairs to the glass room. He opened the door and fired a few shots in the air. All we could hear was a rumbling in the bushes that resounded down the hill.

After that glass experience, whenever I was alone, I slept in one of the upstairs bedrooms. On another occasion, I had just come home from the valley and was all alone in the house. I heard some noise downstairs. I went to investigate, but found nothing. I knew someone was out there. I went to my dad's room, pulled out a pistol, and emptied the first chamber in case I accidentally pulled the trigger in my bed. The next morning, I found that someone had tried to jimmy the locks on the front door.

My older sister was off to college, which meant that I had a Falcon station wagon all to myself. My parents had enrolled me in Notre Dame High School as a 10th grader, and I was going to be on a swim team with my former competitors.

Unfortunately, they remembered that I had been in the same grade as they were in. Now, however, I was a year behind them. I had a car, but no friends, and I was the only 10th grader with a car. Interestingly, Jerry Mathers, the Beav, attended the school, and he was in the same grade as I. He must have been a held-back kid, too. He had his own group of friends, though, and in fact we never even talked.

I tried out for the football team, but that did not work. So my life consisted of school and swim practice for a while. Then came an incident that officially started my career at Notre Dame. It happened in a Latin class taught by a Catholic brother who was the head of discipline. He always joked around with the kids, and his famous line was "What egg were you hatched from?"

He was in the back of the room one day when he made that comment to a boy. I was in the front of the class, and I quietly said to a boy next to me, "What egg were you hatched from?", referring to the brother. The boy laughed. In an instant, the head of discipline was above me. He said, "Write down what you said." I quickly wrote exactly what I had said. I received a slap on the head and was told to report to detention until further notice.

The classroom was completely silent. After the bell rang, my classmates gathered around me to ask what had happened and to tell me I would be dead meat. That afternoon, I reported to detention and, of course, the brother was the monitor. As he excused everyone from detention, only the head of discipline and I were left. I was ready to get banged around. He called me up and said I had a lot of guts to write what I had really said. He knew other kids would not have done that. He added, "Get out of here, and do not come back." One comment, one detention, and now I had friends.

Notre Dame swimming season was about to begin, and I was back in my element. The team was good, having two strong swimmers whom I had competed against for years. They were 11th graders, so I took some heat for being a year behind. (If I had not been held back, I would have been in 11th grade.) Both boys would get scholarships to USC, a swim powerhouse in those days. The team was set, and we could have competed in the CIF finals but came up a little short. Since we all had another year, though, the team looked very promising.

15. Beaver's First Date

During the season, I made friends with this dork with black-rimmed glasses. When I had time, I would give him a ride home to Reseda. He used to get to school and back on the transit bus system. One fine day, he met this girl named Stevie from another Catholic school. He wanted to ask her out but had no car, so Stevie fixed me up with her best friend, and we went on a double date. We went to a movie, and my date and I got along very well and ended the night with a kiss. Stevie bypassed all kisses from the dork and was really jealous of her friend. Stevie was cute and only fourteen years old. We could have been brother and sister due to our freckles.

Sometimes I would show up with my mom's Lincoln Convertible, which was really more like a boat than a car. The dork, Stevie, and I would roam around town with the top down and hubcaps flying when we made quick turns. Stevie really did not like the dork and always feared that he may try to give her a goodnight kiss.

Then came the second double date. At that point, I had my own girlfriend. She came from a wealthy family, more of my mom's type. Stevie came from a poor family and had a younger brother, and her mother was divorced. That date became a feud between the boys and the girls led by the couple in the back seat. I am not sure how it started, but both girls ended up leaving the car. Once we had rounded them up, it was a quite ride home. Now, you may be wondering why this is important. I assure you that it is. The dork's girlfriend would make a lifetime impact on me.

In case you have not yet figured out what happened next, Stevie and I started dating later that summer. Stevie had a younger brother named Billy. Her mother had money problems, and at the time she was dating a carefree rich boy from Bel-Air. In fact, without my knowledge, Stevie and her mom had been evicted from their Woodland Hills house and had moved into a two-bedroom apartment in Van Nuys. I considered this to be good news for me because their apartment happened to be near Notre Dame High School. In those days, I did not understand what being poor meant.

The summer was a blast at the beach and was filled with dinners at Bel-Air Country Club and day trips to Balboa Bay Club. We had splendid times at Balboa Bay Club taking out the Lido sailboat with Stevie's girlfriends. Then we would head over to the fun zone and dock at the pier to play games. Unexpectedly, a few months later, the Beverly Hills police showed up at the Bel-Air house with a warrant for my dad. I had gotten a parking ticket for my sailboat.

That was not my last sailing experience. Years later, I was at it again.

One night shortly after our marriage, we were having cocktails and dinner with friends at Marina del Rey. Just outside our table's window was a sailboat for sale. As the drinks took over, the conversations turned to sailing and some of my

experiences. Our friends knew nothing about sailing, so this was a new adventure for them. Stevie and I talked about finances the next morning. The issue was

whether to purchase a couch for our apartment or buy a sailboat. We opted for the sailboat. We would keep the beanbag chair as our couch.

Our new partners knew little about sailing, but the husband was an engineer, so he took over as captain. I became the first officer, which was perfect for me. Every weekend, we went down to the marina for a sail out of the harbor. I also started a

Thursday Happy Hour. We would bring food and booze and take a sunset cruise. My captain became the ultimate sailor and would even maneuver the boat into the dock without using the outboard motor. I was the exact opposite. By the time I would motor into the dock, I would have everything put away for a fast exit. I am not sure if my dad would have approved of the method.

After we had been dating for some time, an incident occurred that made my relationship with Stevie become extremely important. My older brother needed my station wagon, so Stevie and I headed to Beverly Hills in his new Mustang in search of a mansion with hundreds of statues. Coldwater Canyon Boulevard had just one lane, and a lady tried to pass us on the right, causing a crash. Of course, she blamed me, stating that all locals knew that drivers pass on the right. Having to return my brother's first edition Mustang all dented was very unfortunate. Stevie had never met my brother or sister-in-law and was really scared, and rightfully so. Boy did I need my precious girlfriend at that moment. She was my only witness. "Crash Connelly Junior" had just had his second accident.

During the summer that year, I took my second job. My first job at a Howard Johnson restaurant as a dishwasher had not been at all promising. During the first week, the job ended when a waitress came back with a half-eaten meal and told me that I could finish it. I promptly got on the phone and asked our family chauffeur to pick me up. As the chauffeur arrived, I told the manager I was quitting. He responded that I was the best dishwasher he had and that he would not pay me for the hours I had worked. Both the waitress and the manager were shocked when I jumped into the limousine.

That same summer, I decided to take my second job while my family was traveling in Europe. Universal Studios was starting a tour. The initial starting point of the tour in those days was in front of the studio on Lankershim Boulevard. The visitor's tram would go to the top of a hill, passing through a few exhibits, and then proceed down the hill to the sets and sound stages. Midway, there was a stopover with concessions and a set that included an old Model T and a backdrop for photos. My job was at that stopover, cleaning up and helping out with the concessions.

The good part of the job was that I was on my own and was never involved in the frantic work done at the top of the hill. The downside was being the youngest employee at Universal Studios. I did not socialize with the older workers and had some work-related issues, such as when my boss asked me to change the Coke™ canister in the concession. All the canisters looked the same, so I mixed up the Coke™ and the root beer. I created a very interesting brew that was not the most pleasing to drink.

One late Sunday afternoon when there was no traffic on the tour, a private tram showed up. A small party arrived at the halfway point. It was Elvis and Priscilla. They were having a good time at the Model T and asked me to take a picture of them. My shift was almost finished, so I rode with them for the remaining part of the tour. They were surprised that a maintenance boy would be knowledgeable about the sets and the back lot of Universal Studios.

The next summer, I took a job again with the Universal tours. But a lot of things had changed. Gone was the start at Lankershim Boulevard, and the tour began at the top of the hill, rather than the bottom. There was more commercial business involved, and many more bosses. An image that stuck with me from my time on the job was the smoke from the first Watts riot. Universal feared that the riot would move up the 101 to the studios.

In keeping with "Crash Connelly Junior" tradition, one morning I clipped a car in the parking lot at the studio. The incident was very minor, thankfully, and I left a note. It became a two-fold problem, though; first because the other car belonged to an administrative assistant at the studio who made a big deal of the scrape. Second, I was driving my dad's grandmother's pride and joy, the Rambler.

16. Beaver's Newspaper

By this time, my dad was producing all kinds of shows, such as *Ninety Bristol Court* (NBC), three continuous half-hour episodes about three families living in an apartment complex. One of the shows was called *Karen*, about a girl who was sixteen years old and drove a Falcon convertible. Yes, I had an older sister with the same name who drove a Falcon.

Some of the other shows from that period included *The Munsters*, *Blondie*, *Pistols and Petticoats*, *Going My Way*, and *Calvin and Colonel* (a cartoon with the voices of Amos and Andy). My dad was active in producing, creating, or writing more than 20 shows over the course of his career. He also worked on a few movies. The stars he worked with included Gene Kelly, Ann Sheridan, Mary Tyler Moore, Yvonne De Carlo, Fred Gwen, Al Lewis, and Elvis.

By the late sixties, times were "a-changin.'" The country was in the midst of turmoil. Comic family writing had gone out of style, and detective and violence shows were in vogue. Additionally, sitcoms were making their debut. My dad continued to get family shows produced through Universal, but the number of viewers was taking a fall. The studios had begun to produce shows that did not provide family entertainment, which soon affected my dad. Unlike today, television shows then did at least 30 episodes a season.

One thing that time did tell was that good producing and writing would always return eventually. I look back at the series finale of the Beaver show, called the "Family Scrapbook," which was the first sitcom written with episodes from the past. The wrap party for *Leave It to Beaver* was not over by a long shot. There were more series to come, when the cast had gotten older, plus a new movie, and the original show syndication, which at the time of this writing goes well into 2020. Dads, kids, grandkids, and great-grandkids still benefit financially from the Beaver. Others continue to benefit from *The Munsters* shows and remakes that are still going. Beaver has remained a crucial part of my life, even since I turned seventy.

I had a good friend and neighbor who was a TV icon for L.A. television: George Fishbeck, the weatherman for ABC, and probably the most beloved man in all of Southern California.

George and our families spent a good deal of time together, going out to dinner and relaxing around our pool. One day, he suggested that I do a newspaper interview about my past. At first, I said no because I was in upper management for a subsidiary of a Fortune 500 company. The company had no idea about my background. He finally convinced me to do it for my kids.

The writer showed up for the interview, which lasted a few hours. As we were walking to the door, I commented that he did not seem to believe my story. He gave me a vague look, and I handed him a book titled *The World According to Beaver* about the show. A week later, I received a call from him to request a second interview, this time with a photographer. A lesson business management had taught me was to listen, to think, and then to speak.

My wife had sat through 4-hours of interviews and, per my request, had remained silent. The writer turned to her at one point and asked, "What do you think of the new *Beaver* show?" Then came my shock at her reply about Jerry Mathers: "Poor little wimpy Beav has grown up into big wimpy Beav." She added, "Rick was always getting in trouble, doing deviant things."

Months later, I was traveling back from St. Louis on business. The next morning, I went out to get the newspaper. The front page headline read, "Gee, Wally, It's the Real Beav." I went back in the house and asked my wife if anyone had called about a story. She replied, "There is a small article about you."(It was actually pretty big.)

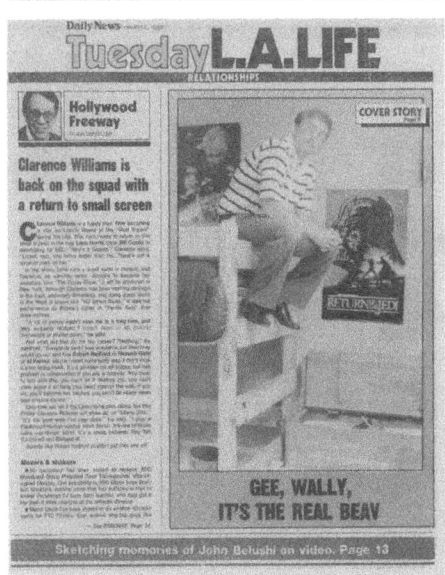

So, of course, the first thing I did was to go down to the local 7-Eleven, buy out the newspapers, and hope that someone would recognize me. When I arrived at the office, my administrator asked, "Whom did you kill last night?" My deal with the writer stipulated that nothing about my work be mentioned, but he had tracked down my wife and gotten my phone number. Publishers, Rick Dees, and the Associated Press had called for interviews.

My next step was to go to the CEO's office with the article. He responded, "Fantastic! I am sending it to corporate." As director of marketing for a commercial equipment division, my job was to travel around the country to our various branches to motivate sales representatives. The article was posted at every branch. Salespeople, in general, are not good listeners, but when the real Beav showed up, they listened. Dad had made an impact on my corporate world.

When my friends happen to see a Beaver show, they often ask if I really did all that. I find it amazing that although the show has been airing for more than sixty years and has been seen by four generations of viewers, I am still asked the same questions to this day. My only reply is, "Yes, I did all that dumb stuff. And, yes, I did have the habit of leaving out initial syllables when I talked."

17. Beaver's Bad Day

In 1964, Connelly and Mosher were at it again producing and writing *The Munsters*, which had a talented cast that included Fred Gwynne, Al Lewis, Yvonne De Carlo, and Butch Patrick. Gwynne and Lewis had completed the TV show *Car 54, Where are You?*

Producing *The Munsters* was extremely expensive due to the makeup, the Munsters' cars, and the overall production costs. The show ran for two seasons and 70 episodes. It was nominated for a Golden Globe Award in the category of Best Television Series. It lost to *The Rogues*, which incidentally was cancelled after one year. *The Munsters* remained a fixture in TV and movies, and remakes have appeared in every subsequent decade. The show would be aired worldwide in every language. In 2020, the original shows are still syndicated daily. Thankfully for me, I did not serve as the inspiration for the character of Eddie.

On the other hand, *90 Bristol Court,* the first prime-time sitcom that lasted an hour and a half, was a network disaster. The TV show *Blondie* was canceled in the midst of a bit of drama. A young director, Peter Baldwin, was filming the show and received a call from my dad. He told Baldwin, "No matter what, keep filming." Universal was taking out all the props from the stage, but my dad wanted to film one more show. That final show was never aired. Peter told me that story on the golf course years later. Peter went on to direct such shows as *The Brady Bunch*, *Family Ties*, and *The Wonder Years*, which won an Emmy.

I would hang out at the studio while my dad had productions going on. Many TV shows were going on and production staffs were friendly, maybe too friendly. The series *McHale's Navy* was a hot show at the time. Some of the staff and I would smoke pot together. At one point, some of the guys asked me to go to their ranch over the weekend. I went to my dad's office to ask permission. He answered a firm "no." He said those guys were gay. I replied, "What is gay?" He responded, "They like boys."

My dad was really street-smart and could relate to any situation. When he was young, he enlisted in the merchant marines and traveled the world. He would remark over the years how poor my pot was. He would tell me stories of his travels in the Panama Canal. He would smoke pot and drink tequila there, and they had the good stuff. He also showed his smarts by retiring from the merchant marines when the state put guns on ships prior to World War II. In later years, he instilled two quotes in me. I have never forgotten them: "I raised you to be smart, not dumb" and "Have fun, but think."

That fall, I was back to Notre Dame, and this time I had a true girlfriend to take to the sock hops and proms at the school. I had a date with her every weekend, and during the fall, I would pick her up with her friends from school. She would come up to the Bel-Air house for dinners and parties. When trying to impress or not impress a girlfriend, there was a place in the valley where you could pay $5.00 to wrestle a seven-foot bear. It took me a few minutes to jump in. I had taken judo lessons once, so at least I knew how to fall. Luckily for me, the bear had a nozzle around his mouth. Guess who won: the bear.

Impressing a girlfriend was easy for me in those days. I had a Chevron gas card and could take her to the best restaurants and clubs. Credit cards barely existed. We went to places like Brown Derby, Cock 'n Bull, Bel-Air Beach Club, Balboa Bay Club, and Schwab's. All I had to do was sign my dad's name. All the bills went to the business manager, and my dad never saw them.

Unlike my older brother, I liked being mischievous. I would take Stevie and her friends all around town. One night, we went to the Wax Museum in Hollywood. In the dark monster dungeon, there was a coffin. I decided I would replace the mannequin with myself. A visitor walked by and remarked, "He really looks alive." When I started to move, the screams from the visitors (my audience) pleased me to no end. The staff did not appreciate my performance.

My mother would say, "You are dating someone from the other side of the hill." As is often the case in relationships, I almost always had a disagreement with Stevie. One rainy fall night was our first. Stevie asked me to call her when I returned home. I was driving my grandmother's 3-speed Rambler, making the transition from the 101 to the 405. A sports car cut me off, and I hit a guard rail going about 40 miles per hour. I flew through the passenger side window, head first on to the hood of the car. That's right, there were no seat belts in that model. I can still remember the male sports car driver looking at me. As he drove off, I chased him for about two hundred yards down the road. I do not remember much after that, but I kept repeating to everyone that I had to call Stevie.

The next thing I remember was being on a bed in the emergency room in Encino. According to the medical reports, I was not in good shape. My dad was hovering over me with a famous doctor from Queen of Angels Hospital. They had been at a party together and were feeling no pain. Once the IVs were in place, the doctor started sewing me up. The only problem was that my dad started giving the doctor suggestions. After the first procedure, I was rushed to St. John's Hospital in Santa Monica. While I had been in Encino, someone had made the call to Stevie. She and her mother were in the waiting room and had received my blood-soaked clothing.

The next morning, I awoke at St. John's with doctors and nuns at my bedside. Over the next few days, I underwent a battery of tests. One of them was extremely painful. The nuns hooked me up to a monitor and stuck about 20 needles in my head. The nuns did not care about causing patients pain. They just kept adjusting the needles. They also had to re-stitch my whole face. The recovery time was about a month, and then they did some additional testing with the needles. Each time, I felt like a dart board.

The good news is that I was ready for the swim season after a month; the bad news, we had a new coach. On the first day of practice, the pool heater was not working, and the temperature of the pool was in the low 60s. Our coach demanded that we swim 200 yards in the cold pool if we wanted to be on his team. As boys started diving in, three of us just walked away. He yelled that we would never be on his team. It only took a day for the coach to realize that he had just lost his three best swimmers. The three would become Prep All Americans later that year.

The coach got back at me in numerous ways that year, having me swim back-to-back events that included a 1,500-yard swim, which would always cramp me up. Also, he would hand me detentions that were self-inflicted. Stevie would attend some meets, and I would wave to her during a big lead. But the biggest detention getter emerged when our coach dismissed the divers from a dual meet. The other team showed up with some divers, so our coach asked for volunteers. Now one thing I could not do was dive. From an early age, I had trouble diving. My first of three dives amounted to a flip and, of course, I landed on my back, which led to a zero. Next came a back dive, and another zero. My final dive was a cannon ball in front of the judges, and more detentions.

We were very good that season. Our team lost one dual meet, when the coach decided not to have us swim in our best events. We were always ranked in the Top 5 for our 400-yard medley relay by Prep Sports. At the CIF semifinals, we were in a tough heat and finished third by one second. The coach yelled that we had not made the state finals. At the finals, however, they called for the Notre Dame medley relay, but we had no team there for Lane 3. The coach had never checked whether we had qualified for that event. Ironically, we later learned that we had become Prep All Americans in that event. The Notre Dame yearbook only mentioned my name in the section about the swim team. I must have been in detention during the photo shoot.

The CIF semifinals turned out to be my last competitive swim. At least my swim career had ended on top.

Getting back to my vehicles, after the Rambler's destruction, my dad purchased me a new VW bus, the one with all the windows and the open top, now a classic.

18. Beaver Gets Spelled

A group of us became party animals at Notre Dame. There was a lot going on with Vietnam and rock and roll. I always favored the folk songs from the early days of Peter, Paul and Mary, Kingston Trio, and Bob Dylan. I had attended all sorts of concerts including those of the Beatles and Dylan at the Hollywood Bowl.

The transition to the Rolling Stones, The Animals, and the like was exciting. To add to the excitement, my group of friends at Notre Dame had their own band. Booze was never a problem because the house in Bel-Air was always stocked, not to mention the fact that I had started drinking at the beginning of my teens.

My dad always told Stevie that she was too good for me. I had four sisters, and I think at times, she was like a fifth, and maybe my dad's favorite of all. When she could not afford something, my dad and mom would have a solution. Whether it be an evening coat or a dress or anything of the sort, my sisters had plenty of expensive items to share. On one occasion, Stevie needed an outfit for a special event. My dad told her to come on over to Universal Studios. The next thing she knew, she was picking out an outfit from the costume department. Truly, the girl from the other side of the hill had become part of the family.

Stevie always attended dinners and major parties at our house and at Bel-Air Country Club. There was a party at the club once for my dad's birthday. The booze was overflowing, and I think the only sober person there was Stevie. As we left the club in the VW van, I pushed my older sister and younger brother into the back. They got drunk with Stevie sitting in the front passenger seat. As we made it around the first curve, Stevie yelled back to my brother, "Shut the door!" After a few attempts, he spit it out that my sister had just rolled out of the van. I hit the brakes, jumped out, and ran down the street, yelling "My sister fell out!" Thankfully, she was not feeling any pain and had flown into some ivy.

That year ended with a few memorable events. Car racing was big at the time, and we would block a street after school for a race. The cars would take off, and the police would show up. One time, we took off in the VW bus and escaped. The only problem was the next day in English class, a good friend had to give an oral report. He recounted the entire story of the race and how we had escaped in the VW bus. The teacher, a Catholic brother, was not happy and made us explain the events.

Having conquered neither the English language nor the Latin language, I decided to move on to Spanish that year. For our final, we had to recite the "Our Father" in Spanish. As luck would have it, Stevie had the "Our Father" down pat. She tutored me, but to no avail.

My dad supported Notre Dame by filming projects at the school. One day on campus, I saw him walking into the gym. They were filming the "All-Star Munsters" episode of *The Munsters*. The actual basketball scenes were played by Darrall Imhoff. He was famous for being the starting center against Wilt Chamberlain, who had scored 100 points in a single game.

My junior year of high school was almost over, and I was looking forward to the summer. Out of the blue one day, I was called to the principal's office and was told that I would not be coming back to

Notre Dame for my senior year. The reason they gave me was my attitude. Now I had encountered some bumps in the road along the way, but attitude was not one of them.

As I left the office, the head of discipline met me in the courtyard to congratulate me on becoming a Prep All-American. I proceeded to inform him that I had just been kicked out of the school. "Why?" he asked, and I said I did not know. He replied that I was enthusiastic. He turned red and stormed toward the principal's office.

When my dad requested a meeting with the principal, they told him that I had been suspended for a few days for not having a written note from my parents for missing a half day of school. That was correct. I had taken my parents to the airport for a flight to New York and could not verify my story with a note. My dad was upset at the school, but it was, quite literally, the school's loss: lost income from his filming at the school. I thought that would be my final goodbye to Notre Dame High School, but Stevie would serve as principal there beginning in the late 1990s for a period of nineteen years.

In 2018, Stevie was invited to the Notre Dame High School Night of Honors. For the induction dinner, I found a prom photo of the two of us. The problem was that the coordinator happened to ask me who the boy in the photograph was. She had looked up my senior class photo and found nothing. I had to explain that she could not find my photo because I had not made it to senior year at Notre Dame.

19. Beaver Plays Hooky

The search started once again for a new school. I was used to it. I had completed eleven grades and had now attended eight schools. There was a new prep school located in a rundown old motel in the San Fernando Valley called Montclair. The only requirement to enroll was that you had to play football.

There was an old pool in front of the motel/school that was as green as a Christmas tree. So swimming was not an option. That summer was the start of the Age of Aquarius. My Notre Dame drinking friends were expanding into marijuana and other stuff. Of course, I had the VW van, so I looked the part. I was a rich hippie.

Montclair had a group of students that could best be explained as the Good and the Bad. There were students like me who had no other place to go and students of parents who wanted a so-called prep education for their kids. The school was extremely small, so the classes were composed of all age groups. Of course, I mixed up with the bad kids. Our school was so small that we played seven-man football, and we had to carpool to games because the school had no buses.

My experience at the school became more enjoyable when basketball season started. I became the leading player on a bad team. In our first game, I missed a free throw and lost the game. So at each practice, I would stay after and would not quit until I made twenty straight charity shots. As I said, we were a bad team, but we had a few games with even poorer teams. In one game, I made eighteen straight free throws. We were so bad that I had to play every minute of every game, which was grueling. In the end, I became the most valuable player.

Graduation was going to be a problem due to my lacking Spanish language skills. After one year of Spanish at Notre Dame and another at Montclair, I could not even count to ten in Spanish. Our final report had to be an essay about Spain, so I went to the Spanish Consulate and found a Spanish version of the Rock of Gibraltar. After making a few typos, I submitted my essay and, of course, received an "F." The teacher informed me that I had failed the class. On the last day of school we went to each class, and the teacher would give us our grade on a card. The good news was that I had gotten A's and B's in my other classes.

I had a plan. I waited to receive my Spanish grade last. When the teacher told me the reason why I was going to get an "F," I showed her the other grades on my report card. I told her that her class had been my only problem. She responded that she did not know that I was that smart. So she gave me a "D," and I could thus graduate. It was always good to have a plan.

Near the end of the year, the principal demanded that all seniors who wanted to graduate write an essay about our experience at Montclair. I began writing the night before it was due, influenced by smoking a little pot. The following school day, I read my essay in front of the class with the principal on hand. By the time I had finished, he had tears in his eyes. I felt as if my hard work had backfired when he announced that I had to read my essay again at graduation.

There was a good deal of speculation as to whether I could pull it off. As it turned out, though, I had the full attention of the attendees upon speaking my first line: "When my withered soul landed on the footsteps of Montclair …" Later that night, diploma in hand, I had graduated. After having attended nine schools, I had miraculously made it through high school. My dad rewarded me with a new Chevy Camaro.

Like all hippies, I had to make my way to Haight-Ashbury that summer. But to do so in a Camaro would not have been authentic. My brother let me take his Corvair instead. With a friend, I decided to take the journey on that Saturday night. Late that night, after he had played a gig as lead singer in a band, we headed out. Our first stop was in Santa Barbara, where we picked up two marines in uniform who were on leave from the war. We all got hungry, so we stopped at a restaurant. We were a unique group: two longhaired hippies and two uniformed marines.

As we entered the restaurant, there was a large group of people I would now call rednecks, who had probably been partying that night. They started in on my friend and me as if we were girls. That did not sit well with the marines, and they spouted some choice words to the group. After we ordered, the situation worsened, and the group kept banging on us. The marines returned insults. I recall one person in the group saying that we would never make it out of that town alive.

The manager called the Highway Patrol, and when they entered the restaurant, they walked over to our table. I said to one of the officers, "Are you going to get us out of this mess?" He replied, "Just shut up, or you will be going to jail." By this time, two more Highway Patrol officers had arrived. They walked the four of us to our car, and we pulled out with one patrol car in front of us and one behind us. As we entered the highway, there was a stream of car lights from that group behind us. After a few miles, the cars disappeared, and later the Highway Patrol cars drifted out of sight. All I could think was how lucky we had been that the officers did not search our car.

We did make it to San Francisco, and we dropped off the two marines. We were staying in Haight-Ashbury with my friend, an old partner from a band. Everything was cool, and we were entering the true world of the love experience. One just needed to go to the park and sit on a hill with Ravi Shankar playing music to experience the culture of the times.

Later that week, we drove back through Monterey and down Highway 1, thinking that we would not run into any more groups of rednecks. Highway 1 between Big Sur and San Luis Obispo is a treacherous, winding drive along the ocean. If a car needs gas, the driver has to find the one station on that 50-mile route. When the time came, we pulled into that little Chevron gas station. With my dad's Chevron card in hand, I walked in and asked the attendant to fill up the tank. The attendant asked me if I had read the sign above the door. It read, "NO Hippies." After some convincing, we did manage to get enough gas to make it back to San Luis Obispo.

I never understood how I made it back to L.A. My friend kept falling asleep, and I kept dozing off as well. I still had not recovered from the incident at the start of the trip. During my Haight-Ashbury travels, there had been an episode at our North Hollywood house. I guess one of our neighbors had complained about a speeding Camaro that had left tire tracks on his driveway. The neighbors started a petition stating that it was the fault of the hippies and that I must leave. I was blamed, even though I had not been in town at the time of the incident. Yes, it had been my older brother. I packed my bags and moved on.

When I returned, I had an idea for a script to write on the experience. Once I had completed a draft of the script, the production was filmed mostly on the back of a pickup truck. I was ready to go to Hollywood, so I submitted it to my dad. My dad, as a family comedy producer, was not really interested. One of his executive producers liked the idea, though, so my dad gave him a copy, but nothing happened.

Years later, I went to the Crest Theatre in Westwood to see a movie called *Easy Rider* with Stevie. Midway through the movie, Stevie just gripped my hand tightly, because she had read my script.

In those days, I was a skinny, long-haired kid who wore yellow glasses. When I was at the beach, girls would sometimes think I was Peter Fonda.

20. Beaver Says Goodbye

I was living off and on at my parents' house in Bel-Air most of the time. If the family was not in Europe, we would be off to Hawaii in late summer. One thing I can say about my dad is that he would always choose the best hotels for us to stay in. My older sister and I would spend a good deal of time together partying. She would also try to set me up on dates.

One day, she introduced me to a girl on the beach. She looked alright. She lived in New Jersey and was traveling with her grandmother. That night, when I picked her up at her room, I did a double take. She had long blond hair and was beautiful. We partied with the Beach Boys, and my date experienced what a Hollywood lifestyle was all about. Unfortunately, it was her last night on the island. After a final goodnight kiss, we promised to stay in touch.

Summer was ending, but I had made no plans for college. This was not a good idea given that a Vietnam draft was in place, and I was over eighteen years old. So I enrolled in a junior college and started to take classes. I started with easy classes that included journalism, theater, and physical education. In those days, you had to take PE, so I enrolled in a swim class. The instructor told us that to pass his course, he would time us on the first day of class and our final grade would be based on how much we had improved over the course of the semester. So on that first day, I slowly made my way across the pool. On the final day, the instructor was shocked to see my time. In my other courses, I did not do so well, due to my lack of effort. Really, it was that I rarely showed up for my classes. I received an "A" in swimming, and the rest of my grades were incompletes.

This did not go over well with the West Los Angeles Draft Board. Due to the income level of West Los Angeles, the board wanted to keep people from the area from being drafted. They even told me that they would give me another semester to get my school credits in line. Of course, I failed again. So I received my draft board letter to go downtown for a physical.

My dad came up with a great idea involving a doctor in Beverly Hills. The eye doctor wrote a report stating that I had double vision. The draft board physical was quite an experience, with a bunch of lectures first and then the testing. I was prepared to show the documentation that could keep me out of the draft. During the final phase that day, a sergeant stamped each candidate's qualification. To my surprise, mine read "1-A." I had been deemed physically fit for a future in Vietnam.

My dad came back with the idea that I should join the coast guard to stay out of the army. He had some contacts who could make that happen. With many of my friends being considered 1-A, there was always the possibility of heading to Canada or figuring out other ways to avoid being sent to Vietnam. One night, I drove with some friends to a free antiwar office that had support lawyers. A lawyer reviewed my eye file and said she would send a letter to the board.

A few weeks later, I received a letter requesting that I report back for another physical related to my double vision. The only way that double vision can be detected during an exam is if a person has it at that time. When I arrived to take the exam, only the doctor and a sergeant were present. During the exam, the sergeant kept yelling at me, "Do you see double now?" Of course, I said no. I could see that he was deeply frustrated with me. He finally went into his office, came back out, and said that there were men in the army who had my condition and others who did not. I replied that I did not want to shoot at someone when I happened to see double. He commented that the board would get back to me.

I had taken the pretest for the coast guard and was waiting to see if I would be accepted. I came home one day and my dad shook my hand with a smile. He showed me a telegram from the Surgeon General of the United States declaring that I was not fit for any military service. To this day, I do not know how I am classified. The West Los Angeles Draft Board had called me to evaluate my college credits a week later. They informed me that I would be drafted because of my lack of credits. When I showed them the telegram, I saw relief in their eyes. One of the regrets I have was that I never got to thank that lawyer from the small support group.

The Bel-Air house was in some disarray due to my dad's business. Family comedy shows were out of style, and detective shows were in. He was no longer the big shot at Universal. No shows, no money. Stevie had graduated high school and was dating other boys due to my lifestyle. For a while, I rented an apartment in the valley with Stevie's old loser, but that came to a crashing halt when I drove the Camaro under a truck (the second major accident for the Camaro). By this time, due to numerous car accidents and tickets, I was left without my Camaro. In fact, my younger sister had the rights to the car. So I was stuck either in Bel-Air or hitchhiking out to the valley.

I had taken a job at a Chevron gas station outside the UCLA side of Bel-Air. The only problem was that I had to cut my hair for the job. Pumping gas, checking oil, and cleaning windshields were not my style.

The manager was a good guy and had been a trumpet player during the big band time in the early 1950s. We would go to his house and smoke grass and listen to his old records. He would always take care of my hours and allowed me to work on customers' cars instead of pumping gas wearing those silly little hats. We had the best of times when we would shutdown the station at night to do inventory.

At a certain point, the manager decided to change my job. I took over as the new tire salesperson, a job that allowed me to let my hair grow longer. It only made sense for me to serve in this new role, due to all the expensive cars that came in from Bel-Air. People trusted me because I lived in their neighborhood. Plus, I had become adept at changing tires. It worked out well for the manager because the station became Number 1 in tire sales in Los Angeles. The only drawback was that I had to attend a special event at the tire factory. That meant a haircut, so that I could look like a Chevron man.

I always had a backup summer job: teaching swimming at Brentwood swim school. My first swim classes had taken place at that school, and the owner had been the coach when I was in 3rd grade at St. John's. The life of an instructor had it benefits: sun and water. The drawbacks were babies and other swimmers peeing on you in the pool. The youngest swimmer to do this to me was six months old. The oldest was 78.

Stevie did not find my drug lifestyle acceptable, nor my no-car situation. So I decided to go east again to find that New Jersey girl. My older sister had a friend living in New York, so I had a place to stay. The problem was I had no idea how to find this girl in Trenton. All I knew was that she went to a Catholic high school.

I jumped on a train and headed there. Upon my arrival, I went to the school and stated my case to a nun. School was out for summer, but she contacted the parents of the girl. Believe it or not, they came and picked me up. I spent the day with her and her parents. They must have liked me because they invited me to a day trip to the New Jersey shore. This posed a complication in that I had been commuting back to New York after each visit to New Jersey. Taking the train late at night is not a good idea. My last trip back to New York had the potential of turning into an awful situation. I had fallen asleep on the train, and when I woke up, it was at the terminal with no one around. As I hit the street around 2:00 in the morning, there were gangs roaming the street and bad circumstances surrounding me. Thankfully, a cab passed by, and I jumped in. That experience was enough to make me want to get out of New York.

21. Don Juan Beaver

Now back in Bel-Air without a car, I decided that Hawaii and school would be a good combination. The decision made a positive impression on Stevie, and we went on a few dates before I left. My dad did some research and got me into Hawaii Pacific College. We flew to Hawaii, and he found me a place to stay at the YMCA and then went back to L.A. The YMCA did not last long. I met a friend, and we decided to rent an apartment. Since neither of us had a car, we traveled by bus or hitchhiked.

There was a great deal of turmoil on Oahu in those days. There were some Hawaiians who liked the mainlanders living there, others who did not, along with the vacationers, the hippies, and the Vietnam soldiers on leave. The North Shore had become off limits for a lot of us due to problems between the mainlanders and the native Hawaiians. There were clashes between the two groups. We always had to be aware of the situations surrounding us. The soldiers created the worst problem with the natives, and there was no love between them.

The one thing I needed was to get a job, as my dad was only paying for rent. I found an excellent job in Waikiki at a dune buggy rental place. My job was to clean the vehicles when they returned. The dune buggies were a big hit in town, but issues arose when they would end up in the ocean. Perhaps the best and worst clients I served were Jimi Hendrix and his band. Every day during his stay, I would have to go to his estate on the ocean and pull them out of the water. The perks included smoking some dope and receiving tickets to his concert.

My favorite activity was hitchhiking to Sandy Beach to bodysurf, but it was hard to get a ride with a surfboard. The people I would meet along the way were interesting. One day, I was picked up by two girls and a guy. We swam naked and wandered through the forest together. The trouble began when we came upon a large estate and a caretaker who was pointing a gun at us. We were out of there in a flash.

Happily, I met a girl at school who lived with her parents at about the halfway point from our apartment to Sandy Beach. Her father was a Vietnam War correspondent who filmed the action there, so we got along well due to my Hollywood background. The girl was an aspiring model. While I was in Hawaii, though, my relationship with Stevie was developing through a good deal of letter writing. I had no phone and could not afford to call her very often. I was on an island that had few modes of communications with the mainland.

Because I had so little money, I would go to Sunday brunches in Waikiki when I had time. I had a jacket with lots of pockets that could store enough food for a week. Then sometimes, I would sit in the lobby of a major hotel and watch for people who had a girl my age checking in. Once the parents headed to the beach, I would somehow introduce myself. My plan worked a few times and resulted in a nice free meal with the parents.

I had a girlfriend but no car. Due to my lack of wheels, I think I became the only person who was homesick living in Hawaii. That Thanksgiving, I told my dad that I wanted to come home and convinced him to send me a ticket. By then, my hair was down to my shoulders, and I had grown a mustache. My dad and Stevie were at the gate upon my arrival. They took one look at me in my white dress shirt and red bandana, and they laughed and walked away. It took awhile for me to get a homecoming kiss from Stevie. My week back in L.A. with Stevie was fabulous, and the love was back. I knew that I had to return to Hawaii, but I was dreading going back there.

I decided in the end that Hawaii was not for me with my empty pockets and so much turmoil going on. I informed my

Hawaii girlfriend that one day I would decide to go home. Another factor that led to my decision to return to California was that I was no longer getting along with my roommate. So before Christmas, I bought a one-way ticket back home.

A week after Christmas, I received a call from my Hawaii girl friend. She said she was at a motel in Hollywood. I told her that I would be right over. The problem was that I did not have a car due to insurance issues. I never went to meet her. The end of the story came about a year later, when I received a Christmas card from her with a photo of her wearing mink and an article from a Hawaii newspaper. She had become Miss Waikiki, which was truly a great comeback after my lack of compassion for her.

22. Wally's Haircomb

My dad asked me to play golf with him at Bel-Air Country Club one afternoon. I showed up a little early to get in some practice because I had never played golf in Hawaii. My hair was still long, and the caddy master came out and was about to ask me what I was doing there. Fortunately, he recognized me and told me that the members at the grill were not happy that a hippie was at the club. I found out later that the club did not like members with long hair. Additionally, my dad's locker was next to the locker of the former governor of California, Pat Brown (the father of former Governor Jerry Brown).

The club decided to allow me to play that day. When my dad showed up, he brought a lady to play with us. She was a talented golfer. As we were putting out on the third green, I asked our caddy for my driver. The lady had a 12" putt as I spoke and missed it. She started yelling at the caddy. Of course, I replied that I had been talking. She would not let the matter go and kept barking at the caddy for the next six holes. Being a fun-loving kid, I quit at the end of nine holes, along with the caddy. At the time, I did not understand why my dad had hooked up with this lady. Only time would tell.

At this point, living at the Bel-Air house was not working. Stevie's car was not the best, so I would hitchhike to the valley to see her and my other friends. Luckily, I solved that problem when I obtained auto insurance, and I got my Camaro back after one year. Because my dad had financial problems, I took another job with the Chevron gas station just below Bel-Air. Once again, I had to face the prospect of cutting my hair and wearing those stupid hats. I would take the graveyard shift at times, so that no one would see me. The middle of the night turned out to be a good shift to work, because it was a dead time. The only customers were people who had been partying that night. Some nights, an old friend would stop by from a famous singing group: Jan and Dean. One of their famous hits was "Dead Man's Curve," a song whose lyrics were about a curve on Sunset Boulevard near UCLA. After the song became a hit, Jan crashed his speeding car into a tree in Beverly Hills. He barely came out of the crash alive and suffered major medical problems.

I once witnessed a collision that showed me how the legal system in our country worked. Back in my VW van days, I saw a hit-and-run accident one night. A pickup truck had been cut off by a red Mustang, and the truck had hit a tree. When I arrived, there were two adults and a girl about ten years of age. Before the ambulances arrived, I sat with the girl, telling her parents things would be alright. I later checked on the girl at the hospital.

A few years later, I received a call from an attorney who wanted me to meet him at the Chevron station for a statement, which I did. I then received a notice to appear in court as a witness. When I was on the stand, the lawyer started questioning me and implying that I did not witness the accident, but that I had instead caused it. He said the reason that I had gone to the hospital was that I had felt bad for causing the incident. He had seen my maroon Camaro at the gas station during my interview with him. He began yelling at me on the stand that I was at fault. I panicked and asked the judge if I could call my father. The request was approved, and I ran to the phone. As I dialed, I stopped and went back into the court. The lawyer kept harassing me and said it was my Camaro that had been involved in the crash. I asked the judge if I could say something. I explained to the court that it could have not been a Camaro because Camaros were first manufactured a year after that accident. It is true that one should never trust a lawyer.

Sometimes, I would take a second job at a Richfield gas station in Brentwood. I would have the afternoon shift and would close the station up in the early evening with another employee named Ken. We came up with some ways to get drinking money for the night. When an older lady would come in with an expensive car, we would check the oil and tell her she needed a quart. We had an empty can of oil and made a buck each time.

In addition, since gasoline was only $.25 per gallon in those days, after a customer would come and request a buck's worth of gas, we would not reset the pump right away. One night, a cool expensive sports car came in with tinted windows. The customer said, "Fill it up." I had the pump at a dollar before I started pumping. As I told him the total and took his credit card, he commented that his car did not take that much gas. I had been caught by a famous actor who knew about cars: Steve McQueen.

23. Wally Buys a Car

One day, my older sister announced that she was going to get married. She had been out of touch with me while she was studying out of state. Stevie and I were going to be in the wedding. A hiccup surfaced when we realized that Stevie was going to be in Hawaii with her friends on the wedding day. Stevie had to choose between Hawaii and Karen's wedding. My dad made the decision easier for her by saying she should go to Hawaii. This meant I had to find a date for the event. My swim school girlfriend from Beverly Hills was off at the Democratic Convention in Chicago with a friend. There were other potential girls, but due to my on-and-off relationship with Stevie, they wanted nothing to do with me.

Karen had asked the Hollywood Priest to marry her at St. Paul's church, but he declined due to his schedule. During the wedding ceremony, though, he did show up and married them after all. The reception was at the Bel-Air Bay Club, which overlooks the ocean. It was the final big bash for my dad and the Connelly family.

The one virtue I had was that I always arrived promptly to my jobs. No matter how much I had partied the night before, my employers knew I would be there. One late night, a friend and I decided to get some food at a 24-hour restaurant in Westwood. We noticed two young girls scantily dressed. We sat down next to them and began a conversation. They had just come back from a concert at the Forum and had hitchhiked that far. They suggested that we visit them at a ranch in Simi Valley, which they described as a really cool place. I had an early morning shift at the gas station the next day, so I left the restaurant. Luckily for me, I never took them up on that offer. Yes, they were part of the Manson clan.

The apartment that we had rented across the street from Montclair had become known by the police. It was good for dope access, not good for potential jail time. Four of us rented a four-bedroom house in North Hollywood. My housemates were friends from my Notre Dame and Montclair days. Due to my job at Chevron, I was the only clean-cut guy. Some of us worked, so we woke up every morning to an alarm: "Here Comes the Sun." Most of us had cars, but we enjoyed having a contest on the weekend. We would break down into pairs and hitchhike to Hollywood. The winning team would be the guys who could make it back to the house with girls. We won.

The Camaro had to go because, in those days, it did not fit the hippie lifestyle. So I was off to visit a famous car dealer, Cal Worthington, which is still around in 2020. You may remember the owner for his crazy animal commercials. This was not the first time I had hooked up with a bear.

I purchased a Ford Cortina, which was supposedly an English racing car. It was ideal, in fact. I was doing some saloon racing with my older brother. We even got a chance to run Riverside raceway with bank turns. During the time trails, I kept losing speed on banks. My brother and my friends just said

I was chicken. We found out later that the carburetor was on the right side of the engine and would suck air through the turn.

Additionally, I did some racing at Saugus Race Track, but not in the Cortina. Saturday nights were all about racing, figures eights, and destruction derbies. At one derby, I had an old Rambler that was dead. Somehow, I got it into running condition for the event. It ran great getting into the stadium but died at the start of the race. There I was in the middle of a field waiting to get hit. Finally, it was one of the last cars, but the winner took me out. The crowd went crazy.

Like most of my cars, this one had encountered a lot of bumps in the road. Stevie and I were in Newport Beach over one summer holiday. I shifted into third gear and the entire shift lever came apart. I drove back to the valley using a screwdriver to shift gears. When I arrived at a dealership, they had no time for us. So I took the gear shift and went into Cal Worthington's office and threw it on the desk. I was out of there within minutes with a loaner car. On another occasion, an oil leak occurred that froze the engine. I never told the car dealer that I had caused the leak when I hooked up a tape cassette to a battery, which caused the oil line to break. The final days of the Cortina will come later.

The house rental with the boys only lasted about six months. I was working in West L.A., and the house was in the valley. When the rent was due, I would find out how little cash my housemates had. Plus, it was not the best situation for my relationship with Stevie, but she still remained in the picture. I could always crash at the Bel-Air house. Due to my dad's financial issues, there were no more maids, cooks, or chauffeurs. I had a great place to sleep, though, in the maid/chauffeur room that was at the end of the house.

24. Beaver the Caddy

I started playing golf again with old friends and a couple of guys from the gas station. We would play all around town. I was also a junior member at Bel-Air Country Club and Lakeside Country Club thanks to my dad's membership.

One day while sitting around in Bel-Air, the caddy master asked me if I could caddie for this foursome because he was out of caddies. I accepted, and off I went carrying two trunks (large, heavy golf bags) and two players on a cart. Even though I had watched caddies while playing with my dad, I had no idea what I was doing, but I at least knew where the next hole was. Later, I was paid $24.00 per loop, which was the minimum. I now had a potential new income. I figured that the combination of four hours of work and being paid cash was a good deal.

So I showed up again, signed in on the sheet, and went down to the caddy yard. I soon found out that caddying is a waiting game. That first day, after four hours, there had been no call. No players, no work. Additionally, caddies had their regular players. All the other caddies had nicknames such as "Snake" and "Golf Ball Eddie." My future name would be the "Member's Son."

After a month, the waiting game was ongoing. I started to figure out the best times and days to work. The benefits of a caddy yard are their food and the many card games going on. Before jumping into the money games, I would watch and figure out the players. The big game at the time was Hearts, but there was no scoring. Because a card player may get a call to the tee, it was all cash and carry after each hand. So you had to read the players. Each hand was like Texas Hold'em. Another game was gin. I learned never to trust a caddy playing for money. I also deduced that it was always crucial to count the cards before starting a hand. Some guys were known for hiding a few cards. It only took me a few times to figure this out.

Caddying did not consist merely of carrying bags or chasing golf carts. We had to know the greens and the yardage and, more importantly, the players. Grantland Rice once wrote, "You learn more about a person in eighteen holes of golf than eighteen years behind a desk." Nothing could be truer because you are dealing with each personality: "No talk, just find my ball", "I cannot hit a shot without you," and, of course, "That was the wrong yardage," or "It does not break." A good caddy never talks about himself or other members. They pay you to listen.

At one point, I figured out that some members started asking for me. Bel-Air was a celebrity club, and my dad's being in the business was a real advantage. I was just a friend to members and really was not star struck. Over the years, I worked for many legends: Dean Martin, Jimmy Stewart, Andy Williams, George C. Scott, Ray Bolger, Howard Keel, and Dick Martin, just to name a few. Then there were the gamblers who played for the big bucks, which included Fletcher Jones and Jerry West. The best loops were the businessmen. They always paid well, took carts, and were less of a hassle and more fun to be around. It was always interesting work. One day, I would be working for the members; the next night, eating dinner at the table next to them.

After six months on the job, I could set my own schedule, show up a little early to play cards, and then make my loop. The two days that I always tried to skip were Tuesday and Friday mornings. They were ladies' days, and I quickly realized their game was not for me. Moreover, I did not think the women wanted a "Member's Son" in their group. The regular guys I worked for also skipped Sunday's mixed couples' golf, later to be called by me "the divorce open." A few times, I would get stuck working that shift when a women's tournament was scheduled. I dreaded when my dad's friend (yes, the lady whom I had walked off the course) would ask me to work on ladies' day. She was a good golfer, but a real pain in the ass.

One particular member was my favorite to caddy for, and he became a future important business figure for me. He played with a great group of guys, at least two times a week. A major problem for caddy masters was a caddy showing up for work drunk or with a bad hangover. When I caddied for my favorite member, my workday started when he brought me out coffee with brandy; after nine holes, it was a gin and tonic. Midway through the backside came the bottle of brandy from the golf bag that we all had to take a shot from. I was one of the few caddies who started work sober and finished drunk.

Eddie Merrins, known as the "Little Pro," was the head pro at Bel-Air and was a good family friend. I started to work for him during a PGA tour on the west coast. Events included the Crosby Pro AM, Pebble Beach, L.A. Open and Andy Williams Open, San Diego. Crosby was always miserable. Between the hail, wind, and rain, it was task and missed cuts, which meant he was out, and there would be no payday.

One of Eddie's best finishes was at the Andy Williams Open. After three days, we were on the hunt for a good finish, and in one of the last groups in the final round. The group included Jack Nicklaus and a young rookie, Hubert Green, showed up dressed from head to toe in bright green. He looked like a small Jolly Green Giant. All Jack's caddy and I could do was laugh. I had done some promotion on one of Jack's teaching videos, and I had some worries about being around the best golfer in the world. The round started out well with Jack and Eddie making birdies (scoring one under par). We came to the six-hole, and Jack hit it fat iron (a miss hit) into the front bunker. Green turned to Jack and said, "You guys hit the wrong golf club" and proceeded to fly the ball over the green and into the water hazard.

On the next fairway, Jack asked what we thought of Green's chances on the PGA tour. I commented that he would disappear. Eddie said that he would probably win once. Jack commented that he was a player and would be successful. After 20 PGA wins and two major champion wins, I told Green the story. He replied, "Jack Nicklaus really thought I was a player."

Neither Jack nor Eddie could keep up with George Archer's blistering round. Andy Williams was a member at Bel-Air. So Eddie received a good deal of TV time, with good images of his caddy. In light of Eddie's strong finish, I had expected a good tip, but it never arrived. On the drive home, Eddie would call Bel-Air asking if he could play the next tour event because he was in the top 10. He was off to Hawaii minus his caddy and did not make the cut; therefore, there was no payday.

25. Lumpy's Car Trouble

The week after the Hawaii tournament was the Bob Hope tournament. The Sunday before the tournament, Eddie said, "I will meet you on Monday at Indian Wells for a practice round." I replied that I would be working for Andy Williams that week. He retorted that I was going for the big bucks. Yes, I was. I formed a relationship with Andy.

One year, I had to drive Andy's Rolls Royce to Pebble Beach for the Crosby Pro Am Golf Tournament. On the way, on the Interstate 5, I got pulled over for speeding. I had an old drunk caddy in the passenger seat. Of course, the officer asked for my registration, so I moved over to the glove compartment. First I pulled out a sheriff's badge from Palm Springs with Andy's name on it, then a package of ZigZags. After a little more searching, the officer just told us to get the hell out of there.

That week, it rained like crazy, so Andy decided to fly up on Wednesday. I had four days with a Rolls Royce convertible. I was staying with some hippies in town, and we partied and drove the Rolls around town each night.

The only problem was I could never figure out how to fill up both tanks. By the time Andy arrived, both tanks were on empty. He remarked, "Don't you know how to fill a Rolls?" I replied that we had only Jaguars, Mercedes, and Lincolns.

The tournament ended without much success. I asked Andy if I could drive the Rolls back that Saturday night. I pulled onto Highway 1 and, not thinking, headed south. Anyone who knows Pebble

Beach knows the best route is to head north towards Salinas. Going south takes you to Big Sur, and there is no turning back for 60-plus miles. The road is narrow and winding, and the drive is dangerous, even in the summer sunlight. I highly recommend avoiding this route at night in the middle of winter, especially in a Rolls. As you can see, I did survive (after cussing myself out for the next two and a half hours). Andy would never have forgiven me if I had driven over a cliff.

When caddying for a celebrity, there is much more going on than touting a bag. Driving, making special arrangements, and the like, are also part of the job. Two stories from my time working with Andy stand out in my mind. The first relates to the San Fernando earthquake in 1972 and took place during the Bob Hope tournament. I asked my girlfriend Stevie to join me that Saturday, and I booked her a flight. The earthquake caused her flight to be cancelled, so late that Friday night I decided to drive to pick her up.

I was a little late picking her up. We returned back to the desert in Stevie's VW bug. The problem was that I was going to miss the tee time. Somehow, though, after begging security to let me in, I made it just in time. Andy did not look happy. In those days, the caddies had to create their own yardage books from previous years or walk the course beforehand. The Bob Hope tournament was problematic in that there were four courses. As we strolled down the fairway after Andy's drive, he asked for the yardage to the green. When I told him the yardage, he commented that it looked farther. The ball had come up short. On the next hole, his second shot flew the green. Once a caddy makes two mistakes, he is in trouble and the player has no trust in his decision making. I finally figured out the issue; I was on the wrong side of the course with my yardage book. All those palm trees look alike.

One of my jobs when I worked for Andy was to get the phone number of any beautiful women who followed us for a few holes. I would walk up and ask for their numbers on his behalf. That day after my yardage mistakes, Andy was in no mood to talk to me. So he turned to his buddy and asked him to get the phone number of a girl with a colored top. I glanced over at the girl and realized that he was referring to my girlfriend. I fired back, "Andy, would you like to meet my girlfriend?" Of course, he rushed over to meet her.

One thing I had learned about being a caddy on away tournaments was not to give up the bag until after I had been paid. Andy had to do an interview with Bob Hope and asked me just to put the bag in the Rolls Royce. "No, Andy," I thought. I told him I would come by the house that night.

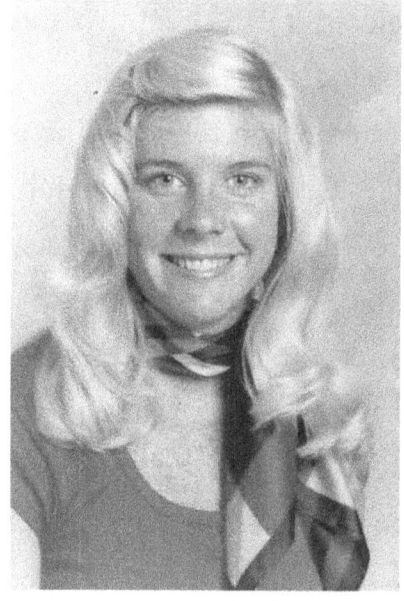

Stevie and I were at a party just down the fairway, and I told her I would be right back. When I entered Andy's house, only Andy and his wife, Claudine Longet, a French-American singer, actress, and dancer were there. After a few glasses of champagne, Claudine and I went out on the grass on the 18th hole. She talked about going up to the falls and swimming nude. She was a beautiful petite woman with a French accent (yes, the same lady who shot Spider Sabich, the Olympic skier). That experience ended my caddying for Andy.

Caddying inspired me to start playing golf again. I had many places to play. As a member's son, I could play at Bel-Air. My dad was also a member at Lakeside Country Club. My dad never played at Lakeside but used the club as a lunch venue because it was across the way from Universal Studios. I enjoyed the fact that the club presumed I was a regular member, not a junior member. I golfed, drank, played cards, and signed the bills, which went to my dad's business manager. Also, there was a group of guys there with whom I would play around town.

Those days became the final days of my Cortina car. I had just caddied for a friend at Bel-Air during the club championship. He outlasted the field in the matched play, winning the final on the 36-hole course. I decided to drive to the San Fernando Valley for some reason. I missed a turn in Bel-Air, went through a white picket fence, and rolled that car down a hill a few times. Miraculously, no damage had been done to my body, but the car was done in. When my dad showed up, he did not ask me if I was alright. He asked why I was wearing his jacket. Yes, I did make it to the Valley that night.

NOT REALLY HOLLYWOOD

Due to my lack of insurance, I purchased an old beat-up Chevy Bel-Air model in Hollywood for $50.00. Thankfully, it started, and I headed to the Bel-Air house. By the time I had hit Beverly Hills, there was a cloud of exhaust behind me. I could not even see out the back window. My mom was not excited to have my new car parked outside our house. The Chevy became known as the "Blue Blur." It looked like a car from a construction derby.

One drawback of caddying is that you risk starving during the winter months. An advantage of working for certain golfers, though, was that they would play no matter the weather. I became a "mudder." Most caddies would not show up on rainy days, but I would. Usually, the situation made for great tips. Also, I would be there waiting on holidays, such as Thanksgiving morning. On one Turkey Day, I packed a bag for a member's son, who was a lawyer, and his father. At the end of the round, the father gave me a big tip. The son, however, promptly took the tip back and stiffed me. Years later, I remembered that big shot lawyer from the O.J. Simpson case: Kardashian.

During the Christmas season that year, I took a job at a Robinson's department store in Beverly Hills. Due to my experience working with kids at the swim school, they had me selling shoes in the ladies and kids department. After a few days of evaluating the right style and fit for highly affluent ladies and kids, I had my own clientele, and Robinson's offered me a full-time job. But I preferred caddying.

26. Price of Fame

I had just finished a loop at Bel-Air when the caddy master informed me there had been an accident, and I needed to go directly to UCLA emergency room. Upon my arrival, I found out that my dad was in bad shape. As he was leaving home, he had crashed his Mercedes into a fence just outside the house. The UCLA police had him in a room, and they claimed that he had been driving drunk. He was out of control, and they pushed him around. In fact, the officers told us to get out of the room. When the doctors had evaluated him, we learned that the issue had actually been brain aneurysms. In simple terms, he had an out-of-control blood vessel that leads to the brain. Dad was in critical condition and was not expected to live through the night. One thing about my dad was that he was always a fighter.

Due to the police problem, my brother and I went to the UCLA police department to file a report on the misconduct of the officers. I do not know if the report had any effect on the medical staff, but fortunately, the best doctors went to work on my dad. He spent months at UCLA hospital, and they ended up placing a metal plate in his brain. After his release, he was transferred to other facilities, and finally to the Motion Picture Hospital in Woodland Hills. As he improved, he lost all short-term memory but still had his long-term memory.

After my dad's illness, my mom had no income, and a few of the kids were still living in the Bel-Air house. My older brother took charge of the move from our beloved home, as well as the other repercussions of my dad's memory loss. The family relocated to an apartment on Wilshire Boulevard. My younger brother had started taking the path of my older brother and was getting into a lot of trouble with the law.

Ironically, before the aneurysms, my dad was scheduled to leave the following day for New York to pitch his play *Under Papa's Picture*. Due to his financial issues and back taxes, the Bel-Air house had to be sold, along with the Bel-Air Country

Club membership. My dad's active involvement in creating, producing, and writing for the film industry during the first Golden Age of Television had come to a close. I have never understood why the Academy has not recognized his lifetime of accomplishments and his incredible work, some of which I have listed below, beginning with the radio shows my dad worked on, followed by television shows that he created, co-wrote, or produced.

Amos 'n' Andy Radio, co-writer, 1940 to 1955
Voices: Charlie Correll, Freeman Gosden
Characters: Kingfish, Calhoun, Lightning, Mystic Knights of Sea Lodge

Fabulous Mr. Tweedy Radio, co-writer, 1945 to 1947
Star: Frank Morgan

Phil Harris Radio Show, co-writer, 1948 to 1954

Stars: Phil Harris, Alice Faye

Edgar Bergen and Charlie McCarthy Radio, co-writer, 1952 to 1954

Stars: Edgar Bergen and Charlie as the Dummy

Amos 'n' Andy TV Show, co-writer, 1951 to 1953

Characters: Kingfish, Calhoun, Lightning, Sapphire

Episodes: 26

The Ray Milland Show (*Meet Mr. McNutley*, original title), TV, co-creator, co-writer, 1953 to 1955

Stars: Ray Milland, Phyllis Avery

Episodes: 75

The Private War of Major Benson, co-writer, 1955
Nominated for Academy Award: Best Story
Stars: Charlton Heston, Sal Mineo, Julie Adams

Bringing Up Buddy, TV, co-producer, co-writer, 1960 to 1961
Characters: Buddy, Violet, Iris
Episodes: 35

Leave It to Beaver, TV, co-creator, co-producer and co-writer, 1957 to 1961
Rated among the 100 Best TV Shows of All Time
Characters: Beaver, Wally, June, Ward, Eddie, Lumpy, Whitey
Episodes: 234

Calvin and Colonel, TV, co-writer, 1961
Animated TV Show, based on Amos 'n' Andy
Voices: Charlie Correll and Freeman Gosden
Characters: Calvin, Colonel, Judge Oliver Wendell

Insight Show, TV, producer, writer, 1960 to 1985
Star: Elwood "Hollywood Priest" Kaiser

Ichabod and Me, TV, co-creator, co-producer, co-writer, 1962
Stars: Robert Sterling, Jimmy Mathers (the Beaver's little brother)
Episodes: 36

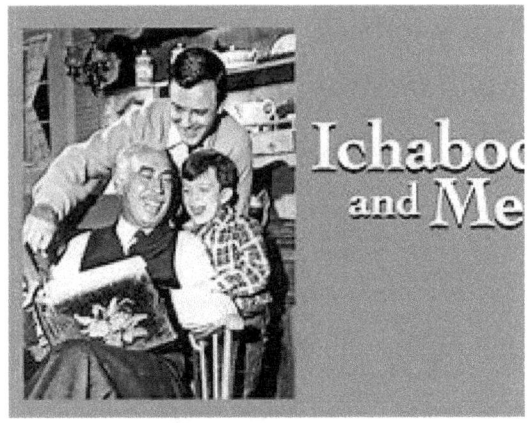

Going My Way, TV, co-producer, co-writer, 1962 to 1963
Stars: Gene Kelly, Leo G. Carroll
Episodes: 30

The Munsters, TV, co-producer, co-writer, 1964 to 1966
Stars: Fred Gwynne, Yvonne De Carlo, Al Lewis, Butch Patrick
Characters: Herman, Lily, Grandpa, Raven, Mockingbird Lane
Episodes: 70

90 Bristol Court, NBC TV, co-creator, co-producer, co-writer, 1964 to 1965
3prime-time TV shows back-to-back
Shows: *Karen*; *Harris against the World*; *Tom, Dick and Mary*
Episodes: 81

Karen, TV, co-creator, co-producer, co-writer
Stars: Debbie Watson, Mary LaRoche

Tom, Dick and Mary, co-creator, co-producer, co-writer
Stars: Don Galloway, Joyce Bulifant, Steve Franken

Harris Against the World, co-creator, co-producer, co-writer
Stars: Jack Klugman, Patricia Barry

Munster, Go Home!, movie, co-producer, co-writer, 1966
Stars: Fred Gwynne, Yvonne De Carlo, Al Lewis, Butch Patrick, Debbie Watson
Characters: Herman, Lily, Grandpa, Cruikshank, Squire

Pistols and Petticoats, TV, co-creator, co-producer, co-writer, 1966 to 1967
Star: Ann Sheridan
Episodes: 26

Far out West, TV, co-creator, co-producer, co-writer, 1968
Compilation from *Pistols and Petticoats*
Episodes: 1

Blondie, TV, co-producer, co-writer, 1968 to 1969
Characters: Dagwood, Blondie, Mr. Beasley
Episodes: 14

Change of Habit, movie, producer, 1969
Stars: Elvis Presley, Mary Tyler Moore, Barbara McNair

NOT REALLY HOLLYWOOD

<u>TV Pilots Unsold</u>

Me and Benjie, producer, 1967

Walter of the Jungle, producer, 1967

Harry and David, producer, 1968

Perils of Pauline, co-producer, 1968

Theater

Under Papa's Picture, play, by Joe Connelly and George Tibbitts, 1972

Star: Eve Arden

Under

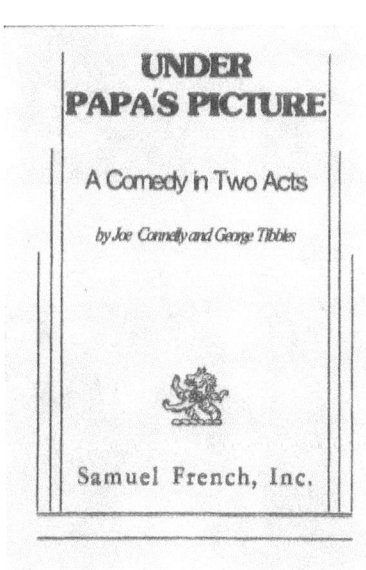

<u>Remakes of original shows:</u>

The Munsters' Revenge, movie, 1981

Still the Beaver, movie, 1983

Still the Beaver, TV, 1984 to 1989

Munsters Today, TV, 1988 to 1991

Here Come the Munsters, movie, 1995

The Munsters Scary Little Christmas, movie, 1996

Major Payne, movie (remake of *The Private War of Major Benson*), 1995

Leave It to Beaver, movie, 1997

Mockingbird Lane, TV special, 2012

When my dad produced a show, it came with a good deal of extra items in addition to photos.

Books

Leave It to Beaver, 1961

Here's Beaver, 1961

Beaver and Wally, 1961

Leave It to Beaver comic books, 1958 to 1963

Leave It to Beaver trading cards

Leave It to Beaver Hasbro board games

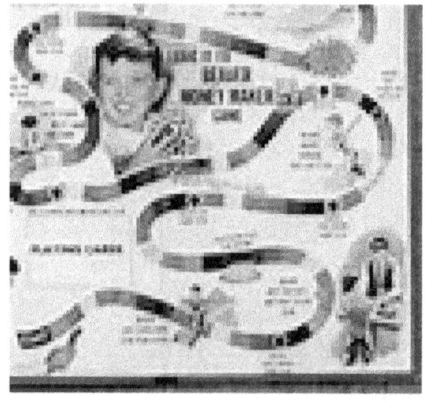

NOT REALLY HOLLYWOOD

Leave It to Beaver lunch box

Leave It to Beaver tee-shirt

Leave It to Beaver pin

Leave It to Beaver CD

Leave It to Beaver cereal

The Munsters comic books

The Munsters dolls

The Munsters cars

The Munsters clocks

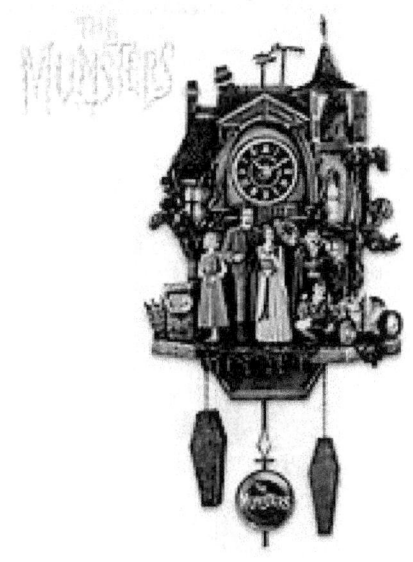

The Munsters slot machines

Munster pinball machines

Munster tee-shirt

The Munsters CD

As of 2021, *Leave It to Beaver* and *The Munsters* are syndicated around the world. Universal claims that *Leave It to Beaver* was the longest continuous show to air on TV. *The Munsters* is in development for a remake movie and TV series. The Golden Age of Television and my dad live on.

27. Eddie, the Businessman

My relationships with club members started to pan out, and one club member asked me to interview for a full-time job. At the time, he was consulting for a company owned by Harry Groman, the L.A. Jewish mortuary king. He had purchased a bus bench advertising company. Yes, I mean those panels on bus benches throughout California. Many of the ads were for mortuaries, and the member purchased the company, so his ads were featured in the key locations. The firm hired me to check out potential new locations and make sure that existing customers had their ads in the right places. There must have been 20,000 benches throughout the state. When the transit company would add a new route, I was right there attending the Metro Transit meeting and then going out to secure the locations. Also, I would wine and dine the transit officials to get insider information. Another perk of the job was a company car.

Mr. Groman never trusted the management of the company. I became a snitch for him. Every week, I would leave the Maywood office, pick up food at Junior's, and go to his high-rise office in Century City to give him information on the management.

Before working in the bench ad advertising field, I would not have thought that it was a cut-throat business, but I learned firsthand that it was. One company in Bakersfield put a bench out when the contract for renewal came up. That company had a friend on a city board. After much debate, the city awarded the new contract to that company for the one bench. After attending a few Bakersfield board meetings, I realized how corrupt business could be. My objections to the board were ignored, and I was asked to leave the meetings. The end result was that we had to purchase that one bench company so that we would not lose our advertising in the city.

As if that were not bad enough, in Los Angeles, there were two companies that competed for the advertising business. A third company emerged and, suddenly, our benches would disappear from key locations. That new company would call our clients and tell them that our ads were not at those locations and offer to advertise with their company. That scenario led to a full-time investigation. The new company would either move our benches from a prime location and replace them with their benches, or use our benches by replacing the ad and company name plate.

This started the "Bench Ad Thief" episodes. Groman had enormous influence in the county of Los Angeles. I started working with the undercover sheriff's department on the case. The sheriffs drove unmarked cars, and one man I worked with had spent six months in jail just to get a confession from a killer. Now the sheriffs were dedicated to the Bench Ad Thief case.

The company gave me video and still cameras. The "Bench Ad Thief" would only work on weekends and mostly in West L.A. During the week, I would find prime intersections and offer the nearby business $10.00 if they reported any action they noticed at a location. That first weekend, my beeper went crazy. The "Bench Ad Thief" was on the prowl. I was able to get photos of him stealing the ads. My days at Georgetown Prep helped in this case because I could develop my own pictures.

Every week, I would take a drive by his business, which was really his home. Sure enough, with my binoculars, I saw our equipment and our ads. I made a call to the undercover sheriff's office, but they were busy. Then, I called the police. When they showed up, I explained the situation and told them that the sheriff's department was involved in the investigation. LAPD wrote the report and allowed me to take photos, but I really think LAPD could not believe what was going on: I had caught the "Bench Ad Thief".

Once I was done stalking the thief, I continued to concentrate on my new full-time job and would also earn a few extra dollars caddying on the weekends. Then the craziest event happened. My mom had to file a restraining order on my dad's golfer's girlfriend, Ann. She had tried to become involved in all our family decisions about my dad's health and finances. The day of my dad's aneurysms, the girlfriend had taken the Mercedes because he had transferred it into her name, maybe because of tax issues. The restraining order did not work because Ann took a job at the Motion Picture Hospital as a nurse. She even wore a wig to disguise herself, and that lead to a custody case in court.

The court case was bizarre. My mom had her lawyer, and Ann had a lawyer from Bel-Air Country Club. The good news was that my dad did not have to attend. My older brother was not liked by my dad. He had caused my mom and dad years of misery, which Ann's attorney was going to take advantage of, so he did not take the stand. When it was my turn to take the stand, I was called a pot smoking, caddying, drinking son. My mom's lawyer did a great job for me and countered that I was a hardworking son who had just started his business career. One of my mom's witnesses was a Superior Court Judge. He talked about how Ann had been suspended from Bel-Air Country Club and her problems with her first marriage. The trial judge and superior court judge did not get along, so there were a few arguments between them. The trial judge passed away before making a ruling.

While my mom remained sober during the court case, she fell off the wagon a few weeks later. She passed away on November 27, 1973 at the age of 56. After the funeral, Ann took my dad out of Motion Picture Hospital and married him in a Catholic church. I had no knowledge of the marriage and am not sure whether any family members knew it had occurred.

Ann was the best thing that happened to my dad at this stage of his life. Despite all my dad's health and financial problems, she must have really loved him. Ann was extremely ascetic. After the wedding, she and my dad moved to Pebble Beach. They purchased a beautiful house on old 17-Mile Drive and a membership at Monterey Country Club. Ann had taken care of all my dad's financial issues and worked with Universal Studios on potential income from his TV shows. The bottom line was that my dad would have an excellent income for years to come and would benefit all of the Connelly clan.

28. Beaver's Ring

Now back to Stevie. After her college graduation, she went on a trip to Europe for the summer with her girlfriends. I was working full-time at the bench ad company and caddying on the weekends. After nine years of dating, maybe it was time to get married. So on the beach in Santa Monica, Stevie gave in, and the decision was made. Stevie, well educated and from a poor family, was hooking up with a boy who had been kicked out of schools, crashed cars, liked booze and drugs, was self-pacing, and was a past Bel-Air brat.

By now, I was living in a studio apartment in North Hollywood with a pull-down bed. My room decorations consisted of panels of the outrageous bench ads. The place was not in the best part of town. One night, I heard some screaming and a gun shot. I opened my door and took a peek outside. From down the hall, a large man said, "Get back inside, if you would like to live." I was out of that place the next morning.

My brother Jay and sister Karen had large, expensive weddings, one at Bel-Air Country Club and the other at Bel-Air Beach Club. With my dad in recovery at the time of our wedding, we were on our own.

How do you pull off a wedding on a low budget? One attribute of my future wife, Stevie, was her creativity. She made our wedding happen on a large scale inexpensively. Stevie was a Catholic school teacher, so we automatically had a church and a folk trio. Now, we just needed a priest. I set up an appointment with the Hollywood Priest, so that we would not have the type of calamity that had occurred during my sister's wedding. I arrived at his Malibu office, and he checked his calendar. He said he was booked that evening, and we were glad that the Hollywood Priest was not going to marry us after all. It was lunch time, and his assistant brought out a nice spread of food. At least he was going to feed me. Then he informed me that the food was for the important meeting that he would have later. After everything my dad had done for him, he would not even break bread with me.

By this time, I was living in a house in Sherman Oaks with our good friend, who was dating one of Stevie's best friends. We set up the rehearsal dinner at a pizza restaurant. The reception was at an inexpensive women's hall. We hired a band and purchased our own booze. The wedding party was large due to the number of Stevie's friends. My family was scattered around the country, and most did not attend. I did have my older brother Jay there as my best man.

Stevie set down the law. If I showed up with alcohol on my breath at the altar, she was out of there. Since we were having a night wedding, the guys decided that a round of golf would keep me out of trouble. My nerves must have been good because I shot 71. The boys and I did have a few drinks, but mouthwash solved my potential issue with Stevie. The ceremony went down without a hitch, although my brother's wife called it a hippie wedding, perhaps due to the folk music that featured Peter, Paul and Mary's Wedding Song.

The wedding reception and celebration afterwards were a little crazy. They felt more like the galas my dad had at the clubs. Some of the Bel-Air members showed up, and Stevie had all her friends there. Unlike a typical wedding, Stevie and I never danced together or performed that traditional cake cutting. The party went well past midnight.

The Bel-Air members had set up the Bel-Air Hotel for our wedding night. Finally, it was time to make our escape, and it was probably the only time I had seen Stevie that entire night. When we got to the car, it was painted in white with everyone's obscene remarks. That was not a problem, but the issues began when I started the car: one big backfire and a cloud of smoke. Our friends had opened the hood and rewired the spark plugs. We made a quick stop at a gas station to try to rinse the car, but that really did not work.

Now, we had to drive from Encino to Bel-Air. The freeway was not our best option because the maximum speed was 30 miles per hour back then. Instead, we went over Sepulveda hill to the rich and famous hotel, and we entered the valet parking with one big backfire. As the valet opened the door, Stevie commented, "We just got married." He replied, "Really, Stevie?" With a bottle of champagne in hand, we were taken to our suite. The valet posed one final question: Did we want him to turn on the fireplace? Keep in mind, it was the middle of the summer. As the door closed, we were out like rocks.

The next day, we were going to drive to Lake Tahoe. Due to the car problems, we did not have time to enjoy the hotel. We were off to one of my old gas stations to fix the car and get it washed. Fondling with spark plug cables was not the best way to start Day Two of our marriage.

Finally, that night, we made it to Tahoe and checked in, exhausted. Luckily for us, we had made reservations for dinner the next night. After a morning in town, we arrived back at the hotel to get ready for dinner. When our first private time since the wedding came, I wanted to take the wrinkles out of my shirt before the honeymooners' act. So I hung the shirt in the shower and turned on the hot water. By the time I went back into the bathroom, it was flooded. We called for towels, and housekeeping showed up and took a look. They said, "We need a water vacuum." The flood had even gone down to the next floor.

The episode did cost us some of our gambling money due to hotel staff tips. My second bathroom flood had proven that the real Beav was alive and well twenty years later.

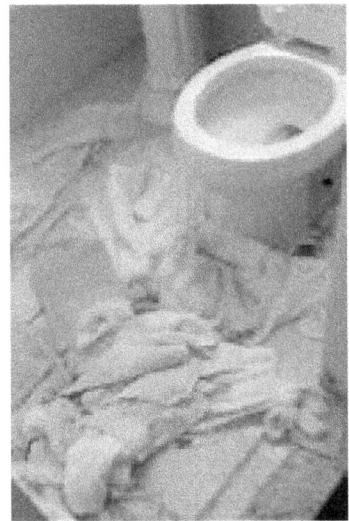

We had rented a nice one-bedroom apartment in the valley. We had a bedroom set, a dining table, and a bean bag for a couch. Stevie was not the best cook, but she came up with one recipe when friends came over. Chicken in wine sauce became the requested meal every weekend.

Now that I had a real job, a company car, and a wife, Gorman decided that we needed to realign the Northern California office and locations. Thankfully for me, Stevie worked as a school teacher, so she had the summers off. Gorman allowed me to hire her as my assistant (at $100 a month). So a week after our wedding, we were off to Northern California. Our expenses were paid, and we had a nice hotel in Sacramento. Stevie would sit by the pool reading *The Happy Hooker* while I did my work. She could not wait for my return each day.

Five times a week we ate fast food and the other two nights, we would have special dinners. Everything went well in Sacramento. The next month, however, we were sent to the Oakland office. There were no good hotels with pools there. Near the Oakland arena, every night the sound of gunshots would alert us. We chose to spend our nights at the hot spots in San Francisco. All in all, it was a good summer.

My work seemed to be going well at the Bench Company, until one morning. Stevie's VW battery went dead. I decided to jump-start it with a push from my car. Well, the bumpers locked, and I sent Stevie back to the apartment. I pulled out the car jack to solve the problem. A little later, I was in the apartment with blood gushing out of my hand. The car jack had slipped, and my hand was in the middle of it. We took a frantic trip to the emergency room, but they could do nothing because of the nerve damage. I made a call to my friend at Bel-Air Country Club, and he set up an appointment with a hand specialist who had worked on Muhammad Ali's hands. The only problem was that it would have taken a few days before I could get in. I needed to have the hand wrapped. So we went to see a doctor Stevie knew for a quick diagnosis. He was like an old country doctor. I explained that I had an appointment with Ali's hand specialist in a few days. The next thing I knew, he was sewing up my hand as I complained. In the end, the specialist was highly impressed by the excellent job the grumpy old doctor had done.

The next few months for the newlyweds were not the best. I could not sleep due to nerve damage. I had to try to sleep in the bean bag chair with my hand held up to the apartment air conditioner. The only other place I could sleep was in the cabin on the bunk of the sailboat. Waves and salty air were the remedy.

29. Beaver's Old Friend

Our Thursday night happy hour continued on the boat and one old friend, Ken, from the gas station days showed up at one point. He had started a job with a commercial upholstery company in Santa Monica. He convinced me that I should interview for a job with them. The job was traveling around the country measuring reupholstering jobs for restaurants. With a new job offer in hand, my days at the Bench Company were coming to an end. In keeping with my driving history, I did have one accident with the company car.

The commercial upholstery company's biggest customer was Sambo's Restaurants, which were scattered around the country. I became a jet-setter, traveling through odd towns in states such as Florida, Nebraska, and Texas.

By this time, Stevie and I had moved into a two-bedroom apartment. The second bedroom was for our family of hamsters. They would keep Stevie company while I was jet-setting. On one occasion in town, I received a call from my friend at work. He asked me to drive with him up to Victorville to a sail plane place. This made sense for him because his father was a private pilot, and he had flown with his dad numerous times. Stevie insisted that she would divorce me if I tried it. Well, I watched my friend take off with a trainer. While waiting, I became convinced that I should give it a try. The first lesson cost only $15.00. As we walked to the plane and glider, the trainer asked what airline I flew for. I responded, "None." Then came the second question: "Are you a private pilot?" I replied, "I have never flown before." As we took off, it was my turn to ask questions. "How long have you been soaring?" His answer was six months. Then I asked, "How long have you been a trainer?" He responded, "This is my first lesson."

About that time, the moment had come to push the button to release the glider. After an incredible moment of silence as we watched the horizon, we did make it back alive and had a few beers to celebrate my accomplishment. One old-timer stated that the sport could be expensive if one rented the gliders. He also told me that one time he had been up in the air and could not get down because of the warm air currents. That was it for me and soaring. Of course, I told Stevie that I had not gone up. The only problem was that she found my flight logbook a few months later.

After about a year, the upholstery company began to have financial issues, due to their sending crews around the country to do remodels for restaurants. In addition, their main customer, Sambo's, was having difficulties. A lesson I learned in the business world was not to let more than fifty percent of one's income depend on a single customer.

So Ken and I started our own commercial upholstery company on Pico Boulevard in Santa Monica. For both of us, the experience amounted to a quick lesson in a start-up business. Ken was the in-house employee, and I was the road man who measured restaurants and took the crews out at night to do the jobs at each location. Based on our experience with the defunct company, we decided to keep our business local in Southern California. One problem business owners have relates to their employees. I found that upholstery workers did not necessarily show up for night jobs.

At the office, you had compressors and staple guns. On the road, you had to spit tacks, which was not very sanitary. You would throw tacks in your mouth and use a magnet hammer to upholster the job. When employees would not show up, their jobs became my jobs. I needed to come up with an alternative to save my mouth. I came up with the idea of using air tanks as a substitute for an air compressor.

As many a businessperson can attest, partnerships can sometimes become one-sided. One person working in the office, and the other traveling constantly and working at night did not work for me. We decided to end the relationship, and I would do the grunt commercial jobs. Now on my own, I was picking commercial jobs with chain accounts and expanding my services. Since I was in restaurants at night, I added to my income by cleaning their greasy carpets. I learned to listen to customers' needs and find solutions for other problems they mentioned.

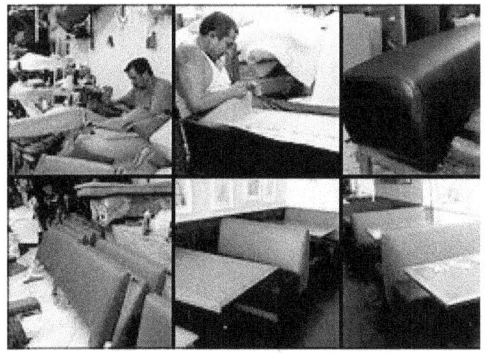

This lesson was all the more significant because I had new obligations at home. Stevie had become pregnant with our first child. So we went house hunting and found our first home. Somehow, with creative funding reports, we made it happen. The pot days were over, and I had become a domestic husband.

Now that we were land owners, we wanted to replace the hamsters because we had a yard and a pool. So we headed to the pound to find a new friend.

As we waited for the big day, we added a dog to the household. Stevie's water broke on her last day of teaching and we had a son, Christopher.

At the pound, we settled on a small puppy that we were told was a German Shepherd. After a few days, our little friend did not look well, so we took him to the vet. The vet explained that the puppy had worms and that he would have to put him to sleep. Stevie would not accept that prognosis. For the next month, we fed the little guy chopped-up hamburger meat and rice. That little pup we named Oliver became a mainstay of our family, but not as a German Shepherd.

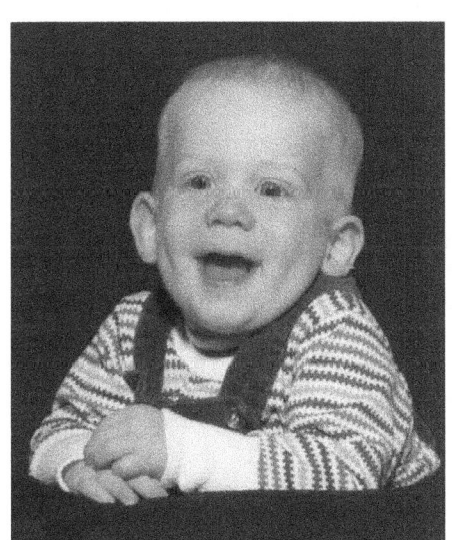

Oliver was the protector of our future family. He was always at the kids' side on walks and activities. If we were in the front yard, he would slide open the back door and jump over a six-foot wall just to be with us.

As an escape artist, Oliver did cause us a few problems. He would get lonely when no one was home and once caused the U.S. postal service to halt delivery to our house. But one postal worker solved that problem. She would leave dog bones in the front door mail slot. When Oliver would make his great escape, he would walk the route with the mail carrier as her protector. The question was how to get him home. He would ride back home in the passenger seat of the mail truck.

One of our neighbors informed us of an episode that occurred when she drove into her garage and heard a noise in her house. She called the police only to find that Oliver had gone through her doggie door (half the size of Oliver) to have some playtime with her dog.

As our kids moved into their teens, Oliver was moving on in age. We took him to the vet because he had a stroke. The vet explained that he was getting old and that he was slowing down, but he would be alright. Stevie asked, "If he is in pain, should we put him to sleep?" As we drove home, I remarked to my son, "If I am ever in the hospital, do not let your mother make a decision on my behalf." Oliver was not just a pet, but a devoted family member.

30. New Neighbors

My business was going well, and Stevie was about to move into the Catholic high school administration. We started looking for a new home because we had another baby on the way. Stevie wanted a brand new house with a brand new pool. The day we moved in to the house, we had to go straight to the hospital. Camryn joined our lives.

Buying a new house was a lot more expensive because we had to add exterior walls and lawns, and of course build a pool. Pool contractors fall into the same category as lawyers and politicians. We decided to use the same contractor as our next-door neighbors. After we had paid for the first installment, and a hole had been built, things spiraled downward. We received a frantic call from our babysitter, who reported that a person was in our backyard hacking up the rebar. The subcontractor had not been paid.

Then the *Los Angeles Times* wrote a story about the fact that our contractor had left seventeen clients with empty holes. Shortly thereafter, an Italian member of Bel-Air Country Club came through for us. My brother had access to a limousine and told me to drive the limo by his office. From the back seat, I would slightly lower the back window and stay there for a few minutes. At that moment, the Bel-Air member made a phone call to the pool contractor. The pool was finished within a month. It was like a story from a Godfather movie.

At a certain point, I started doing jobs on polymer coating furniture and industrial cleanups. I had large contracts at places such as Universal Studios, UCLA, and various management companies. To complete the jobs, I needed financing. With contracts in hand, I would go to local banks for loans. The problem was the floating interest rates that were in place at the time. The country was in the midst of an oil crisis, and the rates had jumped from 8% to 19% on my loans. Businesses had begun to cut back on their major maintenance jobs.

31. Found Money

My expenses were skyrocketing at work and at home. One day, while I was playing Monday golf at Bel-Air, Ed Merrins offered me a job as starter and caddy master. Now I was juggling working full-time at Bel-Air and running a business. Obviously, that plan was not going to work. I closed the business.

Golf had been an instrument for me from my days of caddying to my time as caddy master and starter at Bel-Air Country Club. My year at Bel-Air Country Club gave me some new insights into golf management: what members expected from a club and how employees were supposed to make playing golf a great experience. The "Member's Son" was a perfect fit for the job. I had been running golf tournaments and making sure the members' demands were satisfied. Now, I was setting up golf games and playing with the members.

Bel-Air Country Club is known for the 10th hole called "Swinging Bridge," my favorite hole in golf. One afternoon, I teed off on the 10th and my first shot landed in the hole. Eddie Merrins wrote an article in the monthly newsletter. Rick Connelly aced the 10th hole; on the 11th and 12th holes, scored birdies (one stroke under par); and on the 8th hole, scored an eagle (two strokes under par), and he could only muster a 76.

I would work the morning shift, which allowed me to play golf in the afternoon. Members would request to fill out their foursomes. My favorite player was "Dandy" Don Meredith, the ex-quarterback and the famous announcer for Monday Night Football. We would play at least two times a month together and sometimes with Joe Nathan. One day, I took Dandy Don to the Los Angeles

Country Club (LACC). I informed him that it was not Bel-Air Country Club and that his antics would not be accepted.

It was midday when we reached the first tee. After the two of us teed off, Dandy was on the tee, and he hit his all-time longest drive. Dandy then let out a big whistle. I looked back, and the members at lunch had all stood up. By the second hole, an employee had come out and asked who had invited him to play. I spoke up, and I was never invited to LACC again.

After a year, I asked for a big raise at Bel-Air Country Club. The board turned me down: 0 yeas and 7 nays. It was the best "no" vote of my lifetime. That did not end my relationship with the club, though. When I was caddying and during twenty years of my business ventures, I was asked to work a golf tournament at Las Vegas Country Club that benefited Guide Dogs for the Blind. Barron Hilton hosted the event at the Las Vegas Hilton across the street from the country club.

It all started when a few Bel-Air members asked me to drive around the golf course with a drink cart. A past Bel-Air pro, Joe Novak, was the coordinator of the tournament and worked with the four-man committee. The job entailed all the scoring and that first year, I jumped in and helped Mr. Novak. I would become a fixture at the event for the next seventeen years and coordinated the event after Mr. Novak passed away.

Having eighty Bel-Air members in Las Vegas was quite an experience. It spanned three days and occurred once a year. The work involved went beyond setting up tee times and scoring the tournament. The four-man committee and I would meet months in advance to make the event work. I would work with the Hilton hotel executive staff and departments due to the fact that their boss hosted and played in the event. For me and the Hilton staff, the tournament was a 24/3 job. We worked around the clock for three days, attending to player transportation, golf bags, security, tee times, and food and drink service. Every Hilton employee was treated well, which was part of my job.

To say the event had its moments would be an understatement. There are a few times that stand out in my mind. When the members flew into Las Vegas, we would provide bus transportation to the Hilton. The bus company only knew that the tournament was called the Seeing Eye Dog. One young lady from the bus company asked me how we were going to get the blind people through the airport. I replied, "They all need to hold hands, and we will sing 'When the Saints Go Marching In' until we get them to the buses." She was relieved when they wandered off the airplane with their drinks in hand.

I recall many episodes with the ladies of the night. On one occasion, I flew across a table when a Hughes executive was allowing a lady to examine his diamond ring. With drinks flying, I grasped her hand. I took the ring and put it into the hotel safe deposit box. My job was to protect. One morning around 2 a.m., we were having breakfast, when a lady of the night asked if she could use my room to take a bath. About an hour later, I headed to the room, and she was taking a bubble bath. I flopped down on the bed and fell asleep. The next morning, my wallet was empty. The word got out to the members on the night shift that I had been ripped off. One of the Italian members, who had been a mainstay from the start in Las Vegas, handled the situation. A few weeks later, I received a letter of apology from her, along with my cash.

Bookkeeping was part of my job because I had to pay off winners each day. I would always have a safe deposit box at the hotel. Additionally, the members would take care of me through tips. One late night, I got to the $5.00 blackjack table and started playing. Luck be a lady tonight, by the early morning hours, I was playing $500.00 per hand. Being drunk, the pit bosses would put up with me and every hour, I would go back to the safe deposit box and fill it with chips. By 7 a.m., the pit boss came up to me and said I was teeing off with Mr. Hilton at 8 a.m. After a quick shower, I headed to the tee and birdied the first hole. Mr. Hilton commented that I would be his partner after that birdie. He and his friend were playing for big bucks, and his partner and I were playing a $5.00 bet. We were tied on the 17th hole when I shanked a ball into the hole and eagled the 18th hole for the win.

That night, the group at a cocktail party talked about my crazy night on the tables. I had no idea how much I had won. When I put on my blazer for the night, I found $100.00 chips in one pocket and $500.00 chips in another. After the cocktail party, I headed to the safe deposit box but was stopped by a group that said I was taking them out on the town. The Hilton staff always had a limo for me, so off we went. After a night on the town, I returned to the hotel and headed to the safety deposit box. The teller noted, "I saw you win a lot last night." In the box, I found eighteen thousand dollars in chips. The good news was that I placed a large deposit on a Lexus for my wife; the bad news, over the years, I have given it all back to the tables.

I had chances to work and play in other out-of-town tournaments. One tournament was in Tahoe for the Carol Shelby Heart Foundation. I had a few jobs for the tournament: scoring, filling in as a player, creating an impossible pin placement for a hole-in-

one, and making sure a Cobra was in the casino. The first three were easy, but the Cobra was a test. There must have been an inch or two of leeway to get the Cobra inside the casino doors. As if that were not bad enough, Carol was watching our every move. The hole-in-one prize was the Cobra.

At the opening dinner, Carol announced, "Whoever wins, I will drive them home in a Cobra." Everyone dreaded the idea of a famous race car driver behind the wheel. That night, Mac Davis wrote and sang a great song about Carol's adventures.

There were always ladies of the night around, and sometimes we would meet for breakfast and listen to their stories. Tahoe airport only handled small planes, and due to the weight of the golf bags, the airline asked if we could take the next flight out. Three of us decided that would be fine if they would pay for us to have lunch in town. One of the three happened to be a lady with whom we had eaten breakfast. At lunch, I found out that she was from Beverly Hills and her dad was a doctor. One night watching the news with my wife, I spotted the lady and commented that I knew her. I got an astonished look from my wife and had to explain. Yes, it was the Hollywood Madam, Heidi Fleiss.

32. Beaver the Magician

After some years, we had to sell our house and move on. I took a real job with a new division of Hoover Company for their commercial division. The time with Hoover supported my future business career. My interview was with a division manager who was a past professional football player from the Green Bay Packers. At the start of the interview, he asked if I would like a cup of coffee and left the room. I looked around his office and saw a plaque of Vince Lombard with the quote, "If you don't think you're a winner, you don't belong here." When he came back, he asked me about my goals. I replied, "Winning is my goal." He walked out of the office, spoke to his assistant, and said, "No more interviews." The lesson that I learned was to look around clients' offices to discover their interests.

Before Hoover would let employees out on the street, they had to participate in extensive training on the equipment and learn how to give a presentation. The presentations were focused on features and benefits of each product. I added a third word, advantages, by creating unique phrases and techniques that would convey a lasting image of the product. At the end of the training, employees had to give a presentation to all their salespeople. The skills I acquired learning how to create a marketing and sales atmosphere would stay with me throughout the rest of my career.

I kept Hoover commercial sales on track on my own, without any corporate direction. At one point, the company sent out a vice president from North Canton, Ohio, to see what I was doing right. We met at a Hoover service center, and that's when all hell broke loose. Before he arrived, I had brought in a problem with a piece of equipment from my largest distributor. The VP caught the last part of the conversation in which I had mentioned that the equipment should be under warranty. He went ballistic and ranted that I did not have the authority to determine what was under warranty. Only a service manager did. At the end of his shouting that I should be fired, I calmly inquired, "Before you fire me, do you want to go on the appointments that I set up?"

My dad had taught me that you always had to have a marketing gimmick to create an image for a new product. We made our first stop with a large distributor, and as I made my presentation, I used my marketing ploy. I threw a quarter on the ground and vacuumed it up. The vacuum had a large object trap so that items would not go through the system. As I opened the trap, I would say, "This vacuum is so good it makes change." I had two dimes and a nickel cupped in my hand and threw them on the floor. That presentation would be hallmarked for years. After our third account stop, the VP looked at me and said, "I have seen enough; let me buy you lunch."

My background in commercial carpet cleaning and business contacts vaulted me as the leading regional manager in the country. My biggest account became Hilton Hotels. The national buyer knew of my relationship with Hilton and promoted my products to all of the hotels.

In those days, Hoover commercial division sold to everyone. I went to the largest potential distributor called National Sanitary Supply (NSS) and asked how we could develop a relationship. Tom replied, "You sell to everyone." I left his office, evaluated his comments, and decided he was correct. A month later, I had another appointment with him, and I gave him a list of distributors that I had taken off our list. Tom said, "You are nuts." All I had asked him for was a meeting at all of his branches, which he approved. I went to each branch and set up the equipment. Salespeople meetings with vendors can be boring and consist mostly of hearing how great their product is. All I did in the meetings was make an announcement. I read a list of the distributors that I had cut off and then added, "Salespeople are always asking what manufacturers can do for them; I now ask what salespeople can do for me." Their sales went off the charts.

After one year, Hoover's new agreement with me was not very satisfying, given that I had led the country in commercial sales. The word got out that I was not happy. Distributors began offering me jobs. NSS wanted me as their National Equipment Manager. I started to negotiate with one of the owners and ended up with a good salary and major incentives. After Tom and I had agreed on terms, the CEO came in and lowered the salary a little bit. He looked at me, and I commented with a smile, "With the incentives, I am going to make a good deal of money." The company even gave me a membership at Mountain Gate Country Club.

NSS was growing through company acquisitions around the country, which meant more salespeople. My incentive programs grew, and I became a major player on the team. After one year, I was overseeing all aspects of the national equipment division. NSS became the largest janitorial distributor in the United States. Tom and I began developing a private label equipment line and became one of the best in the country.

The company growth was incredible. I was doing a great deal of traveling for acquisitions and promoting my division products. Additionally, I added a network of service branches and a parts depot. I had become highly skilled at motivating our salespeople and new companies that we had purchased. My storytelling on the company and product achievements would turn a bad situation into a positive one. By day, it was all work, and by night, a good deal of partying, definitely a trait that I had learned from my dad.

NSS had their own additional way to promote sales. Every salesperson was given a quota for the year. If they made their quota, the company would kick in an all-expenses paid trip for them and their spouse or friend. A person who had never been out of the States could take a trip to Spain, the Caribbean, or Hong Kong, among other destinations. Each month, the company would send out a report to the homes of the salespeople. Legal or not, the incentive did encourage the spouses to get the salesperson to work.

When I traveled to all of the branches, I studied the salespeople's names. Learning the names of two hundred sales people, plus the names of their spouses became quite a task. The members of the management team would each pick several branches and study the names for just those branches. We would have cheat sheets. The worst management situation would be forgetting a name.

Around this time, I was doing some charity work at the California Youth Authority in Camarillo. The prison was for the most violent criminals before their eighteenth birthdays. It was like prison with the two gates for entrance and the pat downs before you entered. I would teach the kids that there were jobs available in the commercial janitorial business when they were released. Each week I would educate boys and girls on how to clean and run the equipment. Every year they would have a dinner honoring people and groups for the kids.

The day of the event, I had spent time with a sales manager calling on the Camarillo State Mental Hospital. When I arrived at the dinner, I had a bad feeling. The guards all had machine guns out, which I had not seen before. The dinner did not go as planned. A three-hour program was wrapped up in an hour. When I got home that night, Stevie met me at the door and said, "You did not go to that dinner tonight?" I replied, "Yes, I did but it was really strange with all the guards with guns, and dinner was rushed." We flipped on the television and realized it was the day the Rodney King verdict had been announced. To add to that, my NSS team would be working on the supermarkets that had been looted.

On one occasion, I went to North Carolina to play at the Michael Jordan Celebrity Golf Tournament. Before I left, my son Chris handed me Michael Jordan playing cards and asked me to have them signed. A potentially serious problem

turned into a fun time at the celebrity dinner, when I made my move. As I walked over to Michael Jordan's table, a huge bodyguard said, "Michael is not signing autographs." I replied, "Tell Michael he cannot play Mountain Gate Country Club during the NBA finals." Michael smiled and asked me to sit down. We talked, and as he signed the cards, I commented, "Pressure does not require you to make a shot at the end of a game, but when your son gives you Jordan cards to get them signed, that's a more powerful kind of pressure." He laughed and asked me who I was playing with the next day. I said Too Tall Jones, and he remarked that he was playing right behind me and would check out my golf game.

NSS was a private company. It was great every year. I would have a meeting with executives for an hour with my budget, and we would move forward. As the company grew in acquisitions, it made sense to go public. The owners sold to a Fortune 500 Company that took us public. Of course, there were changes and major accountability policies on the way. My title would become National Marketing Director. It was a good title with a good salary, but the incentive programs had been eliminated. More executives had to get a hand into the equipment business that Tom and I had handled for years. He and I would agree on decisions, and if we did not agree, we did nothing. I had an excellent staff throughout the country, and Tom was the best boss ever.

It was time to change positions inside the company. I was offered a new creative job as National Special Service Accounts Director. After running the equipment division, I had my final meeting with all the departments, including the Fortune 500 CEO. I reported all our growth over a ten-year period and explained that keeping the equipment under its own team, and accountability separate, was one of the reasons for our success.

Now, with me out, all the other departments wanted a piece of the division. As I walked out of the meeting, our past CEO commented, "Rick is smiling because he knows that we are going to f__ it all up." Sure enough, over the next few years, they lost millions in equipment sales.

Next, I became Major Accounts Director. There was great growth potential in this job, but now I had too many bosses who wanted my piece of the action. I thought it was time to leave NSS, but in hindsight, it was probably a big mistake on my part. I took a job as vice president with another company. The next two years were not the best. I had left a company that was expanding to work for a company that was losing market share. It was time to exit that company.

33. Child Care

Now, with a good job and Stevie beginning work as an assistant principal at a high school, all was well. We had purchased a home in Woodland Hills next to George Fishbeck's house. The kids were growing, and there were good times for all.

We would take the kids to Disneyland, Sea World, and on various excursions. Every other year, we would venture to Hawaii, starting with Oahu, and in later years to Maui. On the trips, we would take a nanny so that Stevie and I would have some time together. It was a good idea, but it never happened. On one excursion, the nanny saved my Camie's life by preventing a fall into a hillside stream. Maui became our vacation destination for over four decades. My son would marry on Oahu in 2017.

Over the next decade, the Bigler house would be the mainstay for my family. The kids would start Catholic schools and participate in the usual kids functions. My obligations at work did limit the amount of time I could spend with my kids. I would leave the house at 6 a.m. and return home just before bedtime, which was not all my fault because my drive to work was via the 101 to the 405 to the 10 to the 110. On a good day, the journey took one hour and a half. Plus, I did a good deal of traveling. Then on weekends, I would get in some golf. The school where Stevie worked was just up the street from our house, and her

schedule kind of fit the kids' schedule. When she would get mad at me, she would say, "I am raising the kids."

I really was not a lame duck dad. I would attend all the school and other functions, such as swim meets, baseball games, soccer games, dance recitals, Indian guide meetings, and Indian princess meetings. Also, Stevie loved throwing parties for the kids and the adults. Come summer, there was always time for trips to Hawaii or Balboa Island.

Two of my favorite family lines came from my kids when they were young. While driving one day, Chris commented to me and Stevie, "Mom, you were really poor, and Dad, you were really rich; now we are neither." Camie was a pretty good swimmer. One time, after she had won a race, she came out of the pool crying and said, "I don't want to swim no more." She did not like the starter shooting the gun, so I explained that I would stand by the starter and have him shoot the gun softly. When the gun sounded, Camie stared at me with the dirtiest look for a few seconds, dove in, and won the race. Her final comment was, "I don't like you no more." It is too bad my dad did not have the chance to use either of those stories.

Like my dad, I continued to love all kinds of sports, especially Notre Dame football. That had started in my early days of going to South Bend, or to the USC game in town. My dad wanted me to go to Notre Dame. In the early 1960s, we went to the coliseum with Father Hesburgh, president of Notre Dame University. Notre Dame with a win would have been the national champion, but USC won on a disturbed call. I had to drive Father Hesburgh to the airport. It was a very quiet drive, which probably marked the end of my attending Notre Dame (ND). After attending games in South Bend, it was time to take Chris to a game. It turned out to be one of ND's famous "Catholics versus Convicts." I would attend games in South Bend for six decades.

 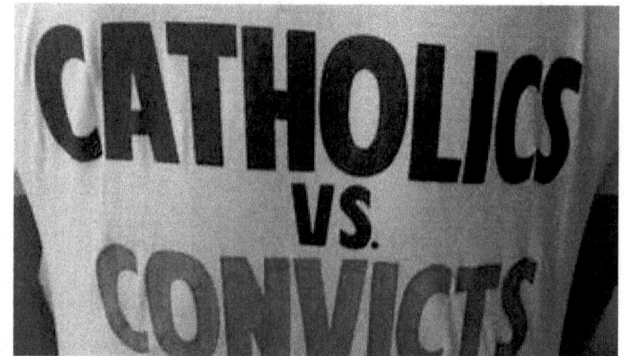

As Chris and Camie reached their teens, we experienced many a wayward moment. Chris and a friend took their new bikes to go play video games and locked their bikes together. When they were ready to leave the arcade, the bikes were nowhere to be found. It was like an old Beaver show. Camie and her friend decided to test her driving skills at the tender age of fourteen. They drove my car right through the garage door. Reminiscent of another Beaver story.

34. Beaver's Long Night

Even though I was a native of Southern California, I had been out of town every time a major earthquake had hit, and I even missed the small ones. When the first San Fernando Valley earthquake occurred, I was caddying at the Bob Hope tournament, as I mentioned, and when the second one happened, I had just flown out of San Francisco. Stevie always complained that I did it on purpose. Once, however, Stevie was off to Las Vegas with her friends. I was left watching my teenage kids over a long weekend. That Sunday, the kids were up till all hours of the night, so I slept on the couch to keep an eye on the front door. Then, boom, the Northridge earthquake happened, and everything began falling apart. In a panic, I tried to find the kids with the heater in the hallway and glass everywhere. We made it out the door and huddled in the front yard. So this time, when Stevie returned, I complained that she had done it on purpose.

At the time, I was vice president of a chemical company that did floor and food prepping business with over a thousand supermarkets. People needed food and supplies, and my job was getting them open for business. Back in my NSS days, I had started working with Health and Safety on employee and customer programs. When I was doing seminars on the Right to Know, one issue was moving bleach away from the same isle as ammonia, because it creates a mustard gas. My crews and I started working on the supermarket disasters caused by the earthquake. Every store in the San Fernando Valley wanted assistance day and night. There was an Agoura manager who kept entreating me to come to his store, which was not in the prime area affected by the earthquake. When I finally reached the store, he complained about our service. It was too bad for him if the store only had a minor problem. I shut him up by showing him pictures of my house and explaining to him that I had no time to take care of my own personnel problems.

Our house was a disaster. The china cabinet had gone through the glass doors. There was plywood on the windows, cracks in the walls, cracks around the pool. Fortunately, we had purchased earthquake insurance when we bought our first home and had continued this practice with each house. On the Bigler house, the insurance was costing us an outrageous $3.45 per month. After weeks of waiting, the first insurance representative finally showed up for the interior and exterior of the house. We walked him through the entire house with him taking notes and telling us what needed to be replaced or redone. I was enthused until he added up the costs of the work and told me that the damage did not meet our policy minimum of $15,000. Thankfully, a call to the insurance agent I had worked with for more than fifteen years solved the problem. I just needed to get bids from contractors. The final replacement costs paid by the insurance company totaled over $100,000.

By that time, the kids were in high school and were becoming a challenge. There was drinking, pot smoking, and car accidents. The blame for these activities would inevitably be placed on me. Stevie was the angel person, and I was always the devil blamed for their actions. I would take everything in stride, having been there before; Stevie, being an educator, would become our family's head of discipline. The kids (two years apart) now had their own personality traits as they approached college. Chris was working on the dark side with pot and car accidents (maybe even a little self-pacing like his dad). Camie was more motivated like her mom, but still had her wild side. Of course, all this put a damper on our marriage.

35. Wally's Election

During my corporate days, the family would take the journey up to see my dad in Pebble Beach. I had fallen in love with the area during my caddy days at Crosby.

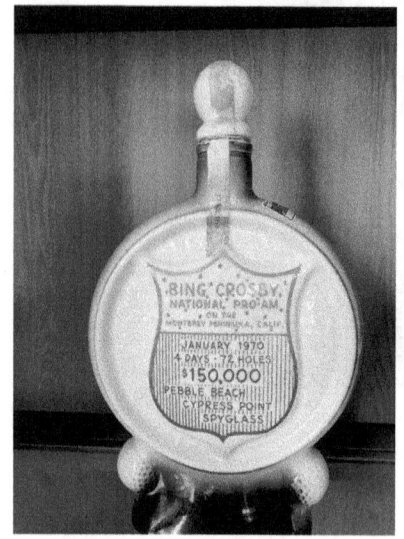

Because my dad and Ann were members at Monterey Peninsula Country Club, I had a chance to get in some good golf at the club. My dad had time to spend with the kids venturing around the Seventeen Mile Drive and showing them his spot. Easter was always a big event.

There were two hiccup occasions. The first occurred when Stevie and Ann had an argument. The kids and I were sleeping in the bedroom. I was awakened by Stevie trying to slide the dresser in front of the bedroom door. She exclaimed, "Ann may kill us tonight."

The second happened when we had decided to head down to Hearst Castle after our stay. My dad remarked, "They have great parties there." He was remembering those old Hollywood days. As we departed from Pebble Beach, Stevie wanted the kids to have chocolate donuts. That was a bad idea for a drive on Highway 1. Chris threw up and Camie followed. With some invasive cleaning, and leaving a blanket on the side of the road, we continued. Luckily, it was a company station wagon that I replaced when I returned to the office.

My dad's second wife died in Pebble Beach in 1992. The funeral was at Point Joe. Ann, who had been a WASP, had requested that two former Flying Tiger pilots distribute her ashes from the air. The group included family and ladies from the club. There were communications with the pilots. There was a lot of chatter from the airport about being in their air space. Just at the moment that the ashes left the plane, a bus full of Japanese tourists arrived. With tears flowing, planes overhead, the airport tower complaining, and tourists clicking cameras, it was a bizarre ending to my dad's life with Ann, which as far as I was concerned had started twenty years earlier.

Ann's will was pretty simple. My older sister would handle Dad's estate and take care of my dad. That meant my dad would now be living in Southern California. She left half of the house to her family, and the other half to Joe's family, which was a big mistake. The families could not get together until the house was sold. One of the other parts of Ann's will was the membership at Monterey Peninsula Country Club. I was the only golfer in the family, and Ann knew that I loved Pebble Beach.

Monterey Peninsula Country Club was built in 1924 and became one of the most distinguished clubs in the country. I needed three sponsors from the club. Luckily, there were three ladies at the funeral, and I got the letters. Then, I had to be interviewed by the membership committee of three. That meant Stevie would attend, which really scared me due to "The Real Beaver" article.

Most of the meeting went well until one man started complaining that the club had too many nonresidents. Stevie then stepped in and said, "Rick has two major loves: his children for whom he will do anything, and golf." I wondered what the committee was thinking when she left her name out of the list.

The next procedure was a photo of us that would be posted for thirty days. The posting was for all members to review in case they would like to complain. Fortunately, I knew no members and was a vice president of a company. Even more fortunate was the fact that they did not know my background.

36. Beaver's Team

Based on my knowledge of the corporate world and my experience playing business golf, in 1996, a headhunter convinced me that I should write a book, because young adults starting their business careers did not know how to act on the course. The headhunter must have thought it was in my genes to be a storyteller like my dad.

So I began writing my first book. My background in caddying and playing customer golf gave me keen insights into the do's and don'ts on the course. I started to write on my original personal Apple computer. I learned "You've Got Mail" and how to send documents.

The only problem was my "California English," which was well-documented from the Beaver stories. A friend and fellow member of Mountain Gate Country Club took on the task of making my writing readable.

Contents

	Introduction	7
1.	Why Golf	9
2.	Getting To The First Tee	17
3.	Setting Up The Tee Time	33
4.	Game Day	49
5.	The Game...And The Bets	57
6.	Balls In The Air	67
7.	Playing In A Man's World	83
8.	19th Hole	91
9.	Scoreboard	105
10.	Corporate Golf Tournaments	115
11.	Your Company Golf Tournament	141
12.	Etiquette	171
	Acknowledgments	189
	About The Author	191

Now, as author, what in the heck do I do with a manuscript? Publishers were not interested, so my co-writer decided to self-publish. Somehow, we got it done but still had the problem of selling the book. Bookstores such as Barnes and Nobles and Crown were not interested in stocking the book because we had not gone through a publisher. So we developed a Guerilla Marketing plan that I had used during my corporate days. We set up a website and conducted a major public relations campaign. We sent hundreds of media kits to golf publications, retail stores, and even President Clinton.

Well, it worked. We started getting free articles printed about the book in golf and business magazines. In fact, we had to go into a second printing of the book. Due to the response, we started selling to Barnes and Nobles and Crown. When they received requests for our book, we would ship each book to the store. The

book cost us $1.65 to publish, and we sold the books to the bookstores for $19.95 each, the retail price, which was a great gross profit. You always have critics, and I had many over the course of my business career. George Fishbeck put it all into perspective when he told me that if you make 50% of the people happy, you are doing a great job.

The kits that we sent to retailers started to take off. The CEO of Federated Stores sent a letter telling us how much he had enjoyed the book. We took that letter to Macy's buyers, and suddenly the book was in their stores. The best experience was with J C Penny. The head buyer for novelty items in J C Penny stores had grown up watching the Beaver and liked my Hollywood background. Our book became probably the only golf book sold in J C Penny department stores. My dad had struck again.

When you write a golf book, everyone thinks you have knowledge of the industry. So we started a company that did public relations and consulting under the name Marketing Golf Resources. We created a website, and potential customers started calling.

One of the first projects we worked on was a company called Golf Mundi, a group of UCLA kids who saw a future in the internet business. Their spokesperson was Chi Rodriguez, a pro golfer. The team was not the best business organization, but it did educate me on the potential of the web as a marketing tool. This was well before Amazon and the like.

Major golf companies had large budgets and would market their products through television commercials, distributors, trade shows, and magazine ads. Small companies and start-ups with small budgets did not have a clue as to how to promote their products, which was a great opportunity for our new company, Marketing Golf Resources.

Marketing

Golf

Resources

Helping You Do Business Successfully...
In The Golf Industry...
And On The Golf Course

My background in the golf world and ability to create a story around a product, coupled with the public relations background of my co-author, Mark, made for a good team. We began launching companies with extensive programs into the world of golf.

Our company's products included golf club manufacturers, golf software, and even car manufacturers. Every client became a learning experience on their approach to being successful. My corporate days would kick in to play as I looked at all aspects of their businesses. A perfect example was Rawlings Golf, a license of Rawlings sporting goods. I was asked to consult on all their business activities. During my first management meeting at each business, I asked each person to write on a piece of paper their gross profit (GP) on their equipment sales. The range was from 45% to 30%. A shock wave would hit Rawlings Golf when I would tell them 16% GP and would explain that "Sales do not pay bills, gross pays bills."

The next aspect of their business that I would address was inventory. Before the meeting, I had found a number of components for a Shamu driver (heads, shafts, grips, and head covers). The owner's son showed me a marketing effort that they were making at Sea World. My dad's storytelling kicked in, and I recounted, "I have taken my kids to Sea World. It costs about $125.00 to get in the door, rent strollers, feed the kids three meals, buy some beer and snacks, and feed the dolphins. Last on the to-do list was the kids' stop at the gift shop. If my son had come out wanting to purchase a Shamu driver, I would have stuck it where the sun doesn't shine."
I wish that had been the only bizarre story involving Rawlings Golf.

37. Beaver Runs Away

There were major changes coming. A few golf companies wanted me to take full-time consulting jobs, which did not sit well with my partner. Also, he was looking to move east. Stevie had now become the first woman principal at Notre Dame, and our marriage was on the rocks. The kids were in college. I was on my own in business. Stevie and I decided to sell the Bigler house, and she would purchase a three-bedroom condo in Woodland Hills. I made the decision to move to Pebble Beach. I had a country club at which to play golf and took a chance on my ability to drum up new golf business.

I was short on cash, and it took me a couple of months to land my first account. Chris had some problems in Southern California, so he joined me and continued going to school. Camie had broken my heart and was going to USC. It took about a year for golf consulting accounts to come on board. My marketing and public relations accounts included club manufacturers, golf fitness and health, golf games, golf professionals, and even a golf song writer. I also started writing articles for *Golf Today* magazine. By listening to the clients, I was able to pound out a story for them and release it to the golf industry. I had become a player.

"Platinum Concepts could never have gotten off the ground without some pros, such as golf marketing maven Rick Connelly, who taught them an MBA's worth of knowledge about the golf business."
USA Today, January 21, 2002

"Another valued contact of mine in golf biz is Rick Connelly. Rick is a PR person who handled a myriad of golf accounts and is a real pusher."
Golf Today, December 2001

"Rick even suggested an ingenious guerrilla-marketing tactic that paid almost immediately at the show. About an hour before opening, he walked the main floor, offering to set up anybody's display PC with a Mouse Driver with a label of our booth number on top. It was a sweet way of touring traffic from other companies in our direction. Rick was brilliant. Without him, we'd have been tourists at another show, this time with serious consequences." Mouse Driver Chronicles

One company was called the Platinum Concepts. Two Wharton MBAs had designed a computer mouse shaped like a golf driver. This account required me to consult two smart, educated men about the golf industry, a prospect that seemed to have no potential. I quickly understood, though, that the account was not about the mouse but rather manufacturing a product and then marketing the product. They went on to write a successful book about their endeavors.

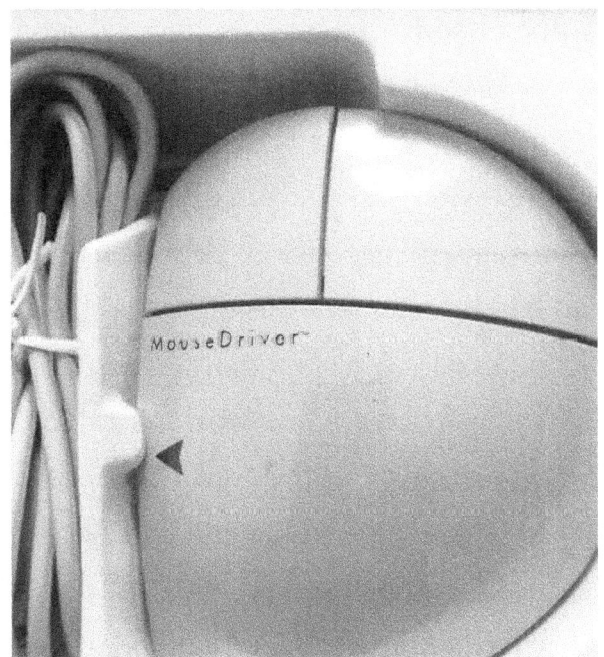

38. Part-Time Genius

One thing I learned about consulting is if you do a good job, the client will not need you after a year. I would tell the customer that from the start. It was a great run for a few years, but the economy was taking a downturn. The golf industry was usually the first to be impacted. That hit my pocketbook. Then I received a call from an old friend from my NSS days.

A San Diego commercial equipment manufacturing company was going through an acquisition. I negotiated a one-year contract to organize the new company as a vice president. During the first week, as I worked on the books, there was a good deal of activity between the old owner and the new owners. Based on my past experiences, I knew there were problems and, sure enough, the deal fell through. Fortunately, my contract was with both parties. The original owner had a family-run business. I knew the owner from my past history with the distributor NSS. He was extremely hard to work with. I had leased a place, and the money was good, so I had no choice but to stay on. During the year, sales increased, and I obtained a profitable original equipment manufacturer (OEM) business with major companies. The problem was that the owner was so difficult to work with. All I really wanted to do was finish my contract and get back to Pebble Beach.

During my time in San Diego, my son had joined me. I was doing a little con-

sulting for a San Diego–based company. The situation worked well for us because I was working full-time, and I was able to turn over all the consulting projects to my son. At first when he had spent time with me in Pebble Beach, he had worked on a few of my golf projects and learned some of my tricks of the trade. At that point, family health became an issue again, and Stevie's mom passed away. But that was not the biggest challenge for me.

NOT REALLY HOLLYWOOD

39. Beaver's Hero

The greatest challenge for me came when my dad passed away on February 13, 2003, at the age of 85 in Newport Beach. Newport was a place where my dad and I had bonded from my early childhood days to my teens. My parents had produced seven children, twelve grandchildren, and six great-grandchildren. The low-key funeral had a few hiccups due to family members wanting their input, but that was always the case with the family. My dad's final resting place was at The Grotto, Holy Cross Cemetery next to my mom.

The media picked up on the passing, and career stories on my dad from every major outlet appeared worldwide. My dad's elegance did not end with his death. New and old television watchers can click on to see his greatness. As I have said and will never cease to acknowledge, our present and future family members will benefit from my dad's lifetime of achievements for many years to come.

40. Beaver's Office Attraction

At an industry trade show while I was with the San Diego company, I met two young lads, again. They had started an internet website company that sold all kinds of stuff from outdoor sheds to office supplies to janitorial products. Their major sales were coming in from sheds that made very little gross profit. What they knew was internet marketing. What I knew was the commercial janitorial market and how to increase gross profit. Janitorial manufacturers had no idea at the time what internet marketing could do to create exposure for their products. In the past, they had relied on print advertising, tradeshows, and the past value of their products. It was an ideal situation in which to create a new internet marketing program. The company was based in San Mateo County in the Bay area, which allowed me to move back to Pebble Beach.

The company was using a wholesale distributor to deliver their products. Again, I had to explain that sales do not pay bills; gross profit does. The gross profit on sheds was at 15%, while janitorial products ran from 35% to 65%, depending on the products. Also, janitorial is a commodity item, while sheds were a one-time purchase.

We started to implement a program to introduce the janitorial manufacturers to the new world. Unlike the traditional methods, our methods could show our future clients the interest customers had in their particular products that they were viewing. Additionally, we could purchase keywords to bring traffic to the Betty Mills site.

My program made money by charging a consulting fee, a percentage of all monies earned on programs and rebates. The program needed to be one that manufacturers could understand. They did not need a program about technology, but one that made sense for them. A perfect example was when I set up a meeting with Georgia Pacific Professional executives at a tradeshow. The boys wanted to attend the meeting and began explaining the technical details of the company. After about fifteen minutes, the president turned to me with a vague look and asked, "Rick, what does this mean to me?" I took over and explained in "street terms" the features, benefits, and advantages of the program. The result was they came on board.

The program included the manufacturers paying a yearly fee for us to promote their products on the website and a percentage rebate on sales. They had advertising budgets, so why not pay us for our services? At the start, I encountered questions such as "Why should I pay you to sell our products?" Our system was new, and "No" was a passing phase. The "No's" became "Yes's" for the next ten years.

Internet marketing strategies had some fun moments. At a tradeshow once, I ran into an old friend from the NSS days. He now was in upper management with the largest janitorial distributor on the west coast. He looked at my badge and said, "Oh no, you are Betty Mills." One of our strategies in those days was to purchase every keyword of products and competitors' products. Keywords and phrases were dirt cheap, because no one was purchasing them from Google. If you typed into a Google search one of our competitors' names, Betty Mills would appear at the top of the page.

We were a major player with Google in those days, and we paid the company quite a bit of money. A trip down to the Google campus was always interesting. I was going down for information to support our company efforts to stay in front of the new technology. The meetings turned into more about how we had become partners with Fortune 500 companies.

The companies that at first had said no were starting to come on board. My job was signing the yearly agreements and working with Betty Mills on support material. We added videos to support our marketing advantages on internet exposure. We could post important information up on the website within hours. When the H1N1 virus (swine flu) hit back in 2009, we were able to have product information to customers within hours. The site went ballistic looking for hand sanitizers and surgical masks. Sales were going crazy, but the real problem was getting products. I applied every one of my 30-plus years in the industry to solve the problem. Besides getting products from our U.S. manufacturers and distributors, I had products flown in from China.

Tech companies are famous for their start-up debt and for bringing in investors. The founders of Betty Mills were an excellent example. They hoped a company would purchase them or go public for the big bucks. I was contacted by a major nationwide player that wanted to hire me as a consultant on internet marketing. That company was making an effort to increase its website exposure. I had past experience with the company, which did over a billion dollars in sales. After reviewing their internet business, I determined that they needed a great deal of help. They sent me a contract that was more like a novel and that had more do *nots* than dos. A few months later after rejecting the offer, I was at an industry party having a great time. A woman executive from the company whom I had known for more than thirty years asked me a question while we were dancing: "If we cannot hire you as a consultant, can we purchase Betty Mills?" An on-looking participant was the president of the company. I replied, "I will talk with the founders."

My first step was to tell Betty Mills there was someone interested in them without telling them which company it was. The next was to see how much they would pay me as a finder's fee. You find out a lot about people when asking them for money that will potentially come out of their pockets. I asked for a finder's fee of 3%, to which one founder agreed and the other did not. He wanted to give me 1/2 %. I finally agreed on 1%, because I had nothing to lose. They really were interested when I told them about the company.

I laid out the sales and marketing plan and let the founders review their financials. The company and executives came to the west coast for meetings. For the next two days, I wowed them with the sales and marketing plan, thanks to my past experience with their company. As always, I tried to figure out what they wanted to hear to support their efforts and how to make them money. At the end of the meetings, they informed us that a financial team would like to come out. The pinstripe suits showed up, including Bain Capital, which owned 60% of Unisource. In

2012, Mitt Romney, a former CEO of Bain Capital, ran for president of the United States.

The Betty Mills founders decided to bring in one of their investors. I did not like the idea because all had gone well during the first day of meetings. Sometimes more is not better. We started by reviewing the sales and marketing plan. I had the Bain people hovering over the table on how I would roll out the program. After that, they started to review the Betty Mills financials. With the day wrapping up, they all decided to go to dinner together, which was a good sign. I had additional work to do to prepare for the next day. I declined the invitation to dinner because too many people can create a bad atmosphere, and too many mistakes are made with booze on the table. At 11:30 p.m., I received an email from the CFO of Betty Mills, asking who should pick up the dinner check. The next day, I could tell from the Bain people's eyes that the night had been a disaster. The Betty Mills founders said it was because of the investor. I found out later that the investor had created problems, but the founders were also to blame. The deal had fallen through.

A little later, the founders were removed from their positions as co-presidents.

I continued my program with the company, but times had changed. I would remain there for another five years because they let me implement my program with manufacturers' partners.

41. The Grass is Always Greener

Monterey Peninsula Country Club gave me many perks for my clients while I worked at Betty Mills. Executives would come west to have meetings. I would ask whether they would like the meeting to take place in San Mateo or Pebble Beach. In most cases, the executives chose Pebble Beach and would bring their golf clubs. I read my own book. I had them on my home field and would just build our personal relationships, without any business talk on the course. By this time, I was playing three times a week with tee times each day at 10 a.m. My vendors, mostly east coast companies, could call me between 5 a.m. and 9 a.m. for conversations.

I had a group of good friends who also played three times a week, rolled the dice for drinks, and played some cards. My golf game was in good shape. I had hit four more holes-in-one and had done well in golf tournaments. We were the first Monterey Peninsula Country Club team to win the Northern California Zone Championship.

MPCC Team Wins 2009 NCGA Zone Championship

MPCC members Richard Bregante, Rick Connelly, Gary Sackett, and Bob Scarpitto won the 42nd Annual NCGA Zone Championship which was held at Spyglass Hill and Poppy Hills on August 31 and September 1.

On the first day, our team was four strokes off the lead and near the middle of the pack after posting a team score of net 14-under-par 130 at Spyglass Hill. The next day, they played exceptional golf in the final round, combining for a score of 20-under-par 124, for a 254 total, in the format that takes the best two of four net scores per hole.

This is a first for MPCC. Congratulations!

(L-R) Rick Connelly, Bob Scarpitto, Richard Bregante and Gary Sackett

I now had Chris living in the area and began making a living through golf. Chris was working as an assistant at Pacific Grove Golf Course and caddying at Pebble Beach and Spyglass Hill. When he had time, we would get some rounds in and, once a year, we played a tournament at the club. The club members and I were having good times. Yes, there were a few dollars changing hands. The group was comprised of more than twenty guys. During the AT&T tournament, we would have a boy's night out with dinner at my place. Not to leave the spouses out, we would also have a yearly dinner at the beach house. This was my big chance to roast the boys with their spouses present. I created a slideshow of golf cartoons about all their antics over the course of the year. The spouses asked in disbelief, "Did you really do that?" They must have enjoyed the dinner and show, because I was the host for the next five years.

6th Golf Group Dinner

Being active in the golf industry has allowed me to play on beautiful golf courses and meet friends throughout the world. My travels in golf have taken me from Mexico to Korea. One of my favorite places is South Korea. The people there remind me of my Irish heritage. They live in a split country and tend to love folk songs and enjoy drinking. South Koreans generally have a special love of the game and, more important, a unique long-term sense of friendship that is extremely special to me.

I guess one cannot talk about golf without a few Tiger Wood stories. I was consulting for Slotline Golf Company when I took a drive over to a Cypress golf range to watch a teenager hit balls. The sound off of the club was something I had never heard before from a professional golfer, and he was just a teen. Three things I remember were how polite he was, his boyish smile and his dedication on every single swing. I was a believer then and to this day. In 2009, when Tiger had his car accident and personal problems, the golf writers made their attack on him. Yes, the story had to be told, but the bitterness was over the top, mainly because he had avoided interaction with the media. At golf trade shows and conferences, I had to speak up.

I related that there was good and bad news surrounding Tiger. The good news for the media was that they had gotten a shot at Tiger; the bad news, it affected the industry. The media would lose income, because they would not be assigned to tournaments, and magazines would lose because of advertising. Additionally, the tour would be affected by a lack of patrons, advertisers, and tour support of the charities. The industry had its fun with Tiger, but the real loser was golf.

42. Beaver's Report Card

My work at Betty Mills was going strong. In between work and golf, I found that I had some time on my hands. Pebble Beach is my heaven, so I decided to write a book about its magnificent golf courses. Yes, it had been done before; I needed to take a different path. I had played all seven of the courses inside the forest numerous times. Why not write a book creating an 18-hole golf course from the best holes in the Number 1 destination in golf? To make it more of a task, I decided to pick holes on each of the courses according to where each one fell on the scorecard. The golf holes did not have to be the longest or toughest, but rather the ultimate setup for a golf course design and scenic enjoyment from 18 holes. This task turned out to be a chore because there were so many fantastic golf holes from which to choose. I soon figured out that I would have to make a second course of eighteen holes. The most arduous task was completing the research on Pebble Beach and the history of each club. I added how to play each hole with the help of my caddy son, Chris.

Contents

Introduction 5
Chapter One: Pebble Beach, Forest and Golf 7
Chapter Two: Number "1" Destination in Golf 11
Chapter Three: Pebble Beach 18, Front Side 13
Chapter Four: Pebble Beach 18, Back Side 17
Chapter Five: The Scorecard 21
Chapter Six: Playing the Pebble Beach 18 23
Chapter Seven: The Pebble Beach Golf Links 29
Chapter Eight: Monterey Peninsula Country Club 32
Chapter Nine: Cypress Point Club 35
Chapter Ten: Spyglass Hill Golf Club 39
Chapter Eleven: Poppy Hills Golf Club 41
Chapter Twelve: The Links at Spanish Bay 43
Chapter Thirteen: Second Pebble Beach 18 45
Chapter Fourteen: The Score Card 49
Chapter Fifteen: Playing the Second Pebble Beach 18
.... 51
Chapter Sixteen: Pebble Beach Golf History Timeline
.... 56
Chapter Seventeen: Author's Par 5 Rankings 59
Chapter Eighteen: Author's Par 4 Rankings 60
Chapter Nineteen: Author's Par 3 Rankings 62
Chapter Twenty: Golf Course Architects/Designers .. 63
About the Author 73

As I have mentioned, I seem to have inherited my dad's genes as a storyteller. Once again, in the case of the Pebble Beach book, a good friend from the club made my California English readable. My idea was to make a tabletop book. I then scheduled a meeting with the best photographer of golf courses in the world and her partner. I assembled the stock photos that I needed from her portfolio. Afterwards, I got a call from the historian of Pebble Beach Company, a person whom I had supported when he wrote a Pebble Beach book. In fact, I headed up the committee when he won the golf book award from the International Network of Golf. Pebble Beach wanted its share of the action. The photos and additional licensing fees were going to break my budget.

Without photos, however, I had no book. As a Member/Owner of Monterey Peninsula Country Club, I requested the photos from them. The tabletop option was out due to costs, so I created a paperback book that began selling on Amazon on Demand. The book did not generate big bucks, but it was in distribution and still is.

43. Last Day of School

My years living in Pebble Beach were coming to an end. I was still married to Stevie. I would call her on our anniversary. She would ask, "How many years have we been married?" Before I could answer, she would tell me. Then she would ask me how many years I had lived in Pebble Beach. My reply would be, "Seventeen." She would quickly respond, "The best seventeen years of my life." That was probably the reason we remained married for more than forty years.

Stevie's health had begun to decline when she started experiencing essential tremors. She was in her eighteenth year at Notre Dame High School and fortieth year in education. She was still living in the same condominium as when I had left for Pebble Beach. The stairs had become a hazard for her, so we purchased a one-story home in West Hills that had all the amenities she wanted, such as a pool and a large backyard for her parties. After her twentieth year at Notre Dame and nineteenth year as principal, the time came for her to retire.

There was one last big bash. Camie decided to get married, and a USC girl does it in style and at her parents' expense with the newlyweds adding some monies. The reception was held on the roof of the Playa Del Rey Marriott with over 200 guests. My dad would have been impressed, because it outdid my brother's wedding at Bel-Air and my sister's at the Bel-Air Beach Club.

My son, Chris, remained in Pebble Beach and was becoming a highly graded caddy. He would marry in Hawaii and purchase a home in the area. His love of golf was just like that of his dad.

My daughter, Camie, always lived in Southern California and earned two master's degrees and a doctorate. She became one of the youngest principals in the Catholic Archdiocese. Her love of education was just like that of her mom.

My life to this point has been a crazy run, from being the real Beaver to participating in swim meets, taking trips abroad, attending school in D.C., partying, pumping gas, teaching swimming, caddying, spitting tacks, living the country club lifestyle, writing, consulting, and finally, marketing on the internet. One thing I know is something I wrote in high school:

NOT REALLY HOLLYWOOD

Look around, don't be down
For ours is a life of love
Come today, come tomorrow
Heaven and earth will stand.

END

Index

Numbers in **bold** indicate photographs

90 Bristol Court 61, 65, 104, **104**

Adams, Casey 15
Adams, Julie **4**, 101, **101**
"All-Star Munsters" 71
Amos 'n' Andy ix, 1, 2, **3**, 61, 99, **99**, 100, **100**, 102
Archer, George 93
Arden, Eve 107
Avery, Phyllis 100

Baldwin, Peter 65
Barry, Patricia 105, **105**
Bavasi, Buzzie 27
Beaumont, Hugh 15, **15**, **23**, 24, **25**, 34
"Beaver and Andy" 21, **21**
"Beaver in the Soup" 21, **21**
"Beaver Takes a Bath" 21, **21**
"Beaver Takes a Drive" 22, **22**
"Beaver Takes a Walk" 22, **22**
"Beaver's Jacket" 22, **22**
"Beaver's Prep School" 23, **23**
Bergen, Edgar 4, 100, **100**
Billingsley, Barbara **11**, **15**, **25**, **33**, 34, **108**
Blondie 61, 65, 106, **106**
Blood, Dr. 33
Bringing Up Buddy 101, **101**
Britt, May 8
Burdette, Lew 27
Burton, Richard 47, **48**

Calvin and Colonel 61, 102, **102**
Carroll, Leo G. 103
Change of Habit 7, 106, **107**
Cohen, Mickey 6, **6**
Connelly, Ann 119-121, 150, 151, **151**
Connelly, Joe ix, 1, 5-6, **7**, 7-8, 10, 11, 13-14, 15, 16, 17-18, 19-20, 21, 22, 23, 24, 26, 27, 28, 29, 30, 31, 33-34, 36-37, 38, 39, 41, 42, 46, 47, 49, 50, 51, 52, 53, 54, 57, 58, 60, 61, 63, 65-67, 69, 70-71, 72, 74, 76, 77, 78, 79, 81, 82, 84, 85, 87, 89, 90, 91, 96, 98-117, 119-121, 122, 123, 139, 140, 145, 150-151, 153, 154, 155, 159, **159**, 167, 169, **171**
Connelly, Kathryn 1, 5, 7, **7**, 10, 11-13, 15, 17, 18, 19, 22, 26, 28, 32, 33, 38, 39, 47, 52, 53, 56-57, 67, 70, 97, 98, 119-120, 159
Connelly, Stevie 56, 57, 58, 67, 68, 70-71, 72, 76, 79, 80, 81, 82, 84, 87, 89, 95, 96, 122-126, **122**, **123**, **124**, **125**, 127-128, 129, 130, 131, 141, 144-145, **144**, 147, 148, 150-152, 156, 158, 169, **169**
Correll, Charlie 1, 4, 6, 47, 99, **99**, 102
Correll, Richard 4, 6, **6**, 10-11, 24, 47-48

Davis, Jr., Sammy 8, **8**
Davis, Mac 137
De Carlo, Yvonne 61, 65, **65**, 104, **104**, 105, **114**, **115**

Disney, Walt 4, **5**, 31, 36
Doggett, Gerry 27
Dow, Tony **10**, 15, **15**, **16**, **22**, **23**, **24**, **34**, **108**, **111**, **114**
Durocher, Leo 27

Easy Rider 76
Edgar Bergen and Charlie McCarthy Show, The 4, 100, **100**
Elmer 49

Fabulous Mr. Tweedy 99
"Family Scrapbook" 61
Far Out West 106
Father Hesburgh 145
Faye, Alice 100
Fishbeck, George 62, **62**, 144, 154
Fleiss, Heidi 137, **137**

Going My Way 61, 103, **103**
Gosden, Freeman 1, 99, **99**, 102
Green, Hubert 92
Groman, Harry 118-119, 125
Gwynne, Fred 61, 65, **65**, **72**, 104, **104**, 105, **109**, **114**, **115**

Hamlet 47
Hancock, George Allan 36-37, **37**
Harmon, Kristin 5
Harmon, Mark 5
Harris Against the World 104, 105, **105**
Harris, Phil 4, 100
Harry and David 107
Here Come the Munsters 109, **109**
Heston, Charlton 4, **4**, 101, **101**
Hitchcock, Alfred 19, **19**

"Hollywood Priest" see Kaiser, Elwood
Hope, Bob 96

Ichabod and Me 103, **103**
Imhoff, Darrall 71
Insight 38, 39, 102, **103**

Jordan, Michael 141-142, **142**

Kaiser, Elwood 38, 39, 87, 122-123, 102
Karen 61, **61**, 104, **104**
Kelly, Gene 61, 103, **103**
Kennedy, John F. 42, 44, 45, 50
Klugman, Jack 105, **105**
Koufax, Sandy 27

Leave It to Beaver ix, 5-6, 10, **10**, 11, **11**, 14, 15-16, **15**, **16**, 18, 20-25, **20**, **21**, **22**, **23**, **24**, **25**, 27, 28, **28**, 30, **30**, 33, **33**, 34, **34**, 46, 51, 61-62, 64, 102, **102**, 110, **110**, 111-114, **111**, **112**, **113**, **114**, 117, 146, 153, 154, 170
Lewis, Al 61, 65, **65**, 104, **104**, 105, **114**, **115**
Longet, Claudine 96

MacMurray, Fred 30-31
Major Payne 110, **110**
Manson, Charles 87
Mathers, Jerry **10**, 11, 15, 16, **16**, 21, **22**, 23, **24**, 28, 30, 33, 34, 46, 54, 62, **108**, 111, **112**, **113**, **114**
Mathers, Jimmy 103, **103**
McHale's Navy 66
McNair, Barbara 106
McQueen, Steve 86, **86**

Me and Benjie 107
Meet Mr. McNutley see *Ray Milland Show, The*
"Merchant Mariner" 23, **23**
Meredith, "Dandy" Don 133-134
Merrins, Eddie 92-93, **92**, 94, 133
Milland, Ray 19, **20**, 100, **101**
"Mistaken Identity" 24, **24**
Moore, Mary Tyler 61, 106, **107**
Morgan, Frank 99, **99**
Mosher, Bob ix, 1-2, 4, 15, 18, 65
Mockingbird Lane 110, **110**
Munster, Go Home! 105, **105**
Munsters Scary Little Christmas 109, **109**
Munsters Today 108, **108**
Munsters, The 48, 61, 62, 65, **65**, 71, 104, **104**, 114, **115**, **116**, **117**, 117

Nicklaus, Jack 34, 92-93, **93**
Nixon, Richard 33, **33**, 42, 43

Osmond, Ken 30, **30**

Perils of Pauline 107
Pistols and Petticoats 61, 106, **106**
Presley, Elvis 7, 23, 31, 59, 61, 106, **107**
Private War of Major Benson, The 4, **4**, 10, 11, 101, **101**, 110

Ray Milland Show, The 19, 100, **101**
Reagan, Ronald 18, **18**
Reeves, Dan 27
Rodriguez, Chi 154
Romney, Mitt 163

Sabich, Spider 96
Sanders, Red 5
Scully, Vin 27
Shelby, Carol 136
Sheridan, Ann 61, 106, **106**
Sterling, Robert 103, **103**
Still the Beaver 108, **108**
Sullivan, Paul 15

Taylor, Elizabeth 47, **48**
Tibbitts, George 107
Tom, Dick and Mary 104, 105, **105**

"Uncle Billy" 24, **24**
Under Papa's Picture 98, 107, **107**

"Wally's Haircomb" 23, **23**
Walter of the Jungle 107
Watson, Debbie **61**, 104, 105
West, Jerry 29, **29**, 91
Williams, Andy 91, 92-93, 94-96
Woods, Tiger 165

www.ingramcontent.com/pod-product-compliance
Lightning Source LLC
Chambersburg PA
CBHW081231170426
43198CB00017B/2727